LIVE IN THE
MYSTERY

MARGARET HUNT

BALBOA.PRESS
A DIVISION OF HAY HOUSE

Balboa Press books may be ordered through booksellers or by contacting:

Balboa Press
A Division of Hay House
1663 Liberty Drive
Bloomington, IN 47403
www.balboapress.com
1 (877) 407-4847

Cover art by © Margaret Hunt

Print information available on the last page.

ISBN: 978-1-9822-5108-6 (sc)
ISBN: 978-1-9822-5109-3 (hc)
ISBN: 978-1-9822-5110-9 (e)

Library of Congress Control Number: 2020913695

Balboa Press rev. date: 08/04/2020

CONTENTS

PREFACE

The events in this book were recorded, collected and hand written in notebooks and journals by me over a number of years. They've been stored in boxes through many moves from place to place. I finally began opening these boxes when I moved into my present home in Denver, Colorado. I rediscovered what I see now as a treasure trove of journals, notebooks and sketchbooks that serve as recorded history. For reasons that weren't clear to me, this writing and drawing seemed important to save through move after move after move. I calculate I've lived in 29 different homes or apartments over the years. I'm glad I trusted that intuition to save these journals. During the long hours I spent re-reading these pages, I began a process of remembering and reflecting on the meaning and impact of some of my seemingly ordinary, and sometimes profound, life experiences.

While I've kept journals for as long as I can remember, I began writing more seriously when my life was being shaken by a series of rapid and unexpected occurrences that I didn't understand and couldn't explain, like the experience of time standing still at 3:15. It seemed important to keep a record for no other reason than to bear witness for myself.

I began compiling these memories in my new home in Colorado with a pot of freshly-brewed coffee and a view of the

Rocky Mountains. It is here, on a sunny day, with a cool breeze carried in through the sliding screen door, that I unpack the box before me in front of the fireplace and settle down to read and remember.

Here I weave together some of my life's most intriguing experiences and reflect on how they've come to impact my life and shape the woman I've become. In hindsight, I can see more clearly the patterns in this weaving and the path unfolding before me. I believe that synchronicity is more than a happy accident. Some say it's God winking at us. Others say it confirms we're part of a connected universe and proof of a connected, unified whole. Certainly, it's an affirmation for me of the mystery of life.

DEDICATION

My father had a profound influence on me. He taught me to recognize the truth by listening to my heart and to communicate without words through the bond of love we shared. He could be a tough-minded taskmaster for sure. I'm thankful he gave so much of himself to me during his all-too-brief presence in my life.

Through my mother I learned patience, endurance and determination. Watching her, I learned how to be calm in the midst of chaos. She taught me management skills. She showed me how to retreat inside myself in silence when I needed to sort things out. Through both of them I learned independence and the power of prayer. I'm thankful for these gifts and their many acts of kindness and forgiveness, in spite of my frequent acts of defiance.

My daughter Nicole has been my touchstone and the center of my adult life who inspires me and challenges me to always be a better person. I dedicate this book to her, my cherished one.

EPILOGUE

These days are woven with faces, places, dreams, and feelings that carry me. I recognize the snapshots and patterns of my own creations along the pathway of this journey, as if to remind me -- wherever I am is where I'm supposed to be.

Each day I participate in both accepting life and letting go, allowing me to enjoy each moment now for the gift it truly is. I cultivate a grateful heart along with the desire to live a meaningful life, and I honor the magic and mystery of life as it meets me and I greet it.

It's with gratitude now that I share snapshots of my story with fellow pilgrims, with friends and family, in both flesh and in spirit.

We are all part of a great love story. There are thousands upon thousands of us on this quest. I feel the presence of my ancestors who've played a pivotal role in bringing me into this world. Sometimes gently, and other times more forcefully, they speak through my dreams and memories. Embraced in love, I celebrate these sweet remembrances.

My heart continues to feel humbled by life's tests and exalted by life's magic. In gratitude, for my ancestors' blood in my veins, this is our collective journey.

The situations that have brought me to where I am today have largely been unexpected and unplanned. My life learning has often been accidental and unusually experiential. Though I know I've had mighty angels watching over me, life hasn't always been easy.

It begins with the same recurring questions that have haunted me all my life. Who am I? Why am I here? For what purpose? Why was I born into this family? What is the purpose of my relationship with this person? Why do I so often feel alone even when I know I'm loved?

I try to get my mind around these questions.

I've been tested, survived nightmares, and witnessed miracles first hand. In the last days of her life, my mother would tease me that I was living a crazy soap opera. I agree that it's felt that way at times.

I was born Margaret Ann in 1951 in Minneapolis, delivered by a female doctor, Isabell Cameron, M.D. on October 3rd. It was just after Bobby Thompson delivered a grand slam home run to win the pennant for the Brooklyn Dodgers in what's become known today as "the shot heard round the world." My father told me it was the happiest day of his life. As an adult I learned it was because of the grand slam home run. Hahaha, that's funny dad.

My family origin is Irish, Scottish, French, Swiss and German. It's Catholic, Lutheran, Jewish, and Christian. I've adopted Buddhism. I'm the eldest daughter with eight siblings. I have six brothers and two sisters, and in spite of the odds in the western U.S., our family is a strong matriarchal one. The name Margaret Ann has been passed down through many generations on both my mother's and father's sides of the family in various derivations, including Anna Margereta. I feel honored by this naming tradition.

I'm told there's Native American blood in our veins on my father's maternal side from a tribe in the Great Lakes or midwest region. And I've had experiences in life which seem to confirm that story may hold some truth.

Professionally, I've used my work experiences to study group dynamics and observe human behavior and try to bring out the best in folks. I enjoy challenges and sometimes find myself waiting in creative anticipation for what may happen next. I'm drawn to new and fresh perspectives and I have an ability to work hard with friends and colleagues to achieve goals.

I have a circle of friends who support me as the woman I am, and together we participate in the process of being and becoming. I take personal risks; I ride the horse, fall off, and get back on again. I dream of riding elegantly and with confidence someday, though that may never happen.

None of us can achieve self-mastery on our own, if ever. For me it's a quest. We all need help from those who inspire us or challenge us, those who tell us when we're wrong and give us feedback so we can reflect and make self-corrections.

Along the way I've found mighty companions for this journey; brothers, sisters, teachers, friends, and lovers. They've helped me know more fully who I am and what I might become. They point out when I'm thinking too small for myself and help me realize a world of endless possibilities.

In my bones, I know myself as a mother, a sister, an artist, and a creative woman fascinated with people and positive ideas. I have an appetite for self reflection that's laced with the wanderlust of a spiritual pilgrim.

So thanks for joining me as I share some of my ordeals as well as transcendent experiences. It's been a crazy ride. Sometimes we will not or cannot understand all that happens to us, so we have to resolve to live in the mystery and dare to be vulnerable.

1

BEGINNING

*"Take if you must, this little bag
of dreams, unloose the cord, and
they will wrap you round."*

William Butler Yeats (1865-1939)

Lightning flashes of summer heat storms, Volkswagens, and the smell of rain and Old Spice bring you back to me.

The screened-in front porch of the old two-story Victorian house on Queen Street in Minneapolis has a rocking chair. I find you there in the middle of the night when the lightning and thunder are shaking the house and awakens me from a deep sleep. My frightened three-year-old self finds my way downstairs to you on the front porch. I climb into your lap and you wrap your arms around me. I feel comfort in your warmth and the smell of your aftershave.

We rock together there and become part of the storm. I see magic and beauty in these storms and in the comfort of your warm embrace.

In those bleak and long Minnesota winters, you turn our backyard into the neighborhood ice rink, teaching us how to skate by holding onto a chair from the kitchen for support and pushing it over the ice. Years later, I visit you in California where you and Mom are living. We sit together in silence, you in your rocking recliner chair. Being in your presence is enough. Words not necessary. What could be hours are passed this way in silence. Mom comes to check on us to find out what we're doing. She's mystified by our ability to pass hours alone together, simply basking in the comfort of one another's presence.

In the California summers of my youth, you install spotlights on the side of the garage, illuminating the backyard for baseball games after the heat of the day has passed. You teach me how to run and hit, and laugh at how I bite my tongue when I throw the ball. You are one of the kids then, understanding us and knowing how to make us happy with simple things.

You take me to my first professional baseball game at Dodger Stadium. They're the Los Angeles Dodgers now, after leaving Brooklyn in 1957, followed soon after by the New York Giants moving to San Francisco. It became a family rivalry. Mom cheering for the Giants, you for the Dodgers.

What a team we are. You buy a bag of peanuts. I crack them open, give you the peanut, and I eat the shells. Life is simple and good.

2

DREAM ANGELS

"Hold fast to dreams, for if dreams die, life is a broken-winged bird that cannot fly."

Langston Hughes (1902-1967)

One night I'm awakened by two sweet old ladies dressed in white gowns standing beside my bed, gently shaking my arm to wake me up. "Come with us," they whisper. "We have a surprise for you."

I can see from their smiles and the glimmer in their eyes that something wonderful is going to happen. I crawl from beneath the covers in my soft white cotton nightgown and hurry away with them.

We fly through the night to my childhood home on Queen Street. From their excitement I feel I'm being let in on an amazing secret. They seem to know me, though I don't recognize either of them. They have that familiar comfort of Minnesota people - trustworthy, clean, honest, and good.

I recognize this familiar place with fondness. It's empty though, without any furniture. At the top of the wooden stairway is a door, and they coax me to open it and go inside by myself. I can see from their faces that a great surprise is waiting for me on the other side. Cautiously, I open the door.

That's when I see him there, waiting for me - my grandpa Armstrong!

Hugh Norman Armstrong. Even after all these years, he still looks exactly the same as I remember. His face is radiant with joy when he sees me, and I run to him immediately.

"It's the little old lady from Pasadena!" he exclaims and laughs as he puts his arms around me, holding me close.

"Come on, let's slide across the floor!" he says in his mischievous voice and sparkles in his eyes. In our stocking feet we run back and forth across the hardwood floors, sliding and laughing in unison. As we play, no words are spoken, only laughter echoes throughout the room. When I realize I'm dreaming, Grandpa tells me it's time for me to go. But I don't want to leave him! In an instant, the spell is broken, and it's over.

Sometimes I close my eyes and go back to the house on Queen Street and slide with him across the floor in stocking feet, and remember how much he loves me.

3
MAKE BELIEVE

"The world is full of magic things, patiently waiting for our senses to grow sharper."

William Butler Yeats (1865-1939)

In Whittier California, we climb fruit trees in the spring and eat ripe avocados right off the tree at the neighbor's house across the street on Gretna. My fifth brother Joe has just been born.

Dad announces the arrival of my new baby brother as I'm perched on the edge of the toilet seat. At four years old, my feet haven't reached the floor yet. I cry when he tells me I have another brother. I want a sister! And I still believe I can have anything I want in life just by willing it to be so. My dad gives me my first spanking that day. Outraged, I serve him "tea" at our make-believe tea party with water I've taken from the toilet where he spanked me. That will teach him a lesson, I tell myself proudly.

I have a best friend now. She lives four houses down the street. She's the only girl in her family too, with several brothers, like me. Her name is Cathy and we play dress up with her mother's old clothes and jewelry. We stuff newspapers in the toes of high heeled shoes so we can wear them when we walk down the street from her house to mine. Grandpa Armstrong has come for a visit. When he sees me dressed this way, he starts singing, "The little old lady from Pasadena" by the Beach Boys.

Freedom from five brothers the summer Joe was born comes in the form of make believe, catching Monarch butterflies in homemade butterfly nets, and hanging out with my new best girlfriend. This is the beginning of many lifelong friendships with girls and women that I treasure.

My brothers and I walk to the corner to catch the bus to St. Mary's catholic school each day. Once we memorize the route, we decide we can walk it. We agree not to tell our parents. We have it timed so that by walking, we'll miss morning mass and arrive just in time for school to start. We're a mischievous bunch.

The busses line up in front of the school each day. A boy

I have a crush on always rides the city bus home. One day I decide to get on his bus so I can sit next to him. After all the kids from my school have gotten off at their stops, the bus driver notices I'm still there. Of course he hadn't seen me on this bus before. He asks me where I live and I give him my address. He pulls into the bus terminal and I see him conferring with other drivers over cigarettes. They plot my route home.

By the time the bus arrives at the corner of my street, it's dinner time. I walk from the bus stop up toward home and see a police car in front of the house, and a worried look on my parents' faces. I confess I deliberately took the wrong bus. I get my second spanking then.

My heart was broken when I learned we were moving from California to Colorado when I was in the 4th grade. I was inconsolable. Our new house is walking distance to Maple Grove Elementary School. There's a piano in every classroom!

Two years later we move again, this time to Bountiful, Utah. I change schools five times in five years and develop the acumen of making new friends wherever we are living at the time. The gift in all of this is the development of an ability to embrace change. I meet my new best friend Jeanna then. She's as skinny as I am! It's the greatest gift ever. She attends public school and wears the most stylish clothes while I'm confined to school uniforms once again. When Jeanna, who's a year older than I am, outgrows her clothes, I benefit from some fabulous hand-me-downs! From her, I gain a sense of style and a shared love of the Monkees and the Beatles, and the end of childhood.

4

WAKE UP

*"If we want our dreams to come true,
the first thing we must do is wake up."*

Margaret Hunt

In a high desert inland city surrounded by towering mountains overlooking a salty lake, a digital clock with glowing red numbers flashes 3:15 3:15 3:15

I bolt upright in my bed, throwing the white down comforter to the floor.

It dawns on me that I'm late for work. I rush to the bathroom as sunlight streams in through the skylight. I brush my teeth in a hurry and splash cold water on my face. I can hear the sounds of city traffic from the loft of my home on Windsor Street. Glancing at the watch on the bathroom counter, I'm surprised to discover it has also stopped at 3:15.

I hear a car engine start up outside as a neighbor shouts goodbye to someone. I rush down the wooden stairs in the early 1900's brick and craftsman-style bungalow and quickly glance through the living room window. A girl wearing a large pink backpack races up the street on her bicycle. I hurry into the kitchen to check the time on the battery operated clock above the sink. The hands are stopped at 3:15. A sense of strangeness envelopes me.

My breathing is shallow as I try to take in this information. I really want to know what time it is and am frustrated that I don't. I dress for work and lock the front door of the house.

Outside, to the east, the peak of Mount Olympus glows pink in the morning sunlight. There's a familiar hum of traffic from the boulevard two blocks away, which informs me that it's the height of rush hour traffic. The bells of the Cathedral of the Madeleine chime eight times. That's helpful information. I put the key in the ignition of my Chevy Blazer but the engine doesn't turn over; the battery is dead.

I race back inside the house to call AAA to jump start my car. The truck arrives, the driver connects the jumper cables, and the engine comes to life. With the engine humming, I glance at the dashboard clock, startled to see it also stopped at 3:15.

I feel a surge of adrenaline hit me and it blows my mind to see the numbers 3:15 again. Breathing fast, my heart pounding, I drive toward the city center, each signal light seeming to anticipate me, turning red before my eyes. Finally, inside the high-rise office tower with the copper colored pyramid roof, the elevator stops on nearly every floor before finally reaching its destination – the 22nd floor. Heads turn as if to acknowledge with surprise, yes, we notice you're late today. This is unusual for me.

I walk into my west-facing office with the view of the lake and stand at attention when I see the clock on the credenza behind my desk -- 3:15. Feeling shock, I make myself take three deep breaths. In that third breath, I notice a package on the corner of my desk encased in brown wrapping paper. Inside I find a note from my friend Allison, "I know you'll enjoy this book." It's Alan Lightman's *Einstein's Dreams*. I flip through the pages randomly stopping on page 53 and read the first sentence,

"There is a place where time stands still."

I'm stunned. What's happening to me?

5

TIME

"Love is what we were born with.
Fear is what we learned here."

Marianne Williamson

I look for Craig, my colleague and friend, and find him in his office, two doors down. He looks up and smiles at me, not seeming to mind me interrupting his morning ritual of coffee and the Wall Street Journal. I tell him about the strangeness of all the clocks stopping at 3:15 this morning -- at home, my watch, my car and office. I read him the line from the book I found left for me on my desk.

"What do you think it means?" he asks, his eyes sparkling in amusement. I read the line from the book once again. A meaning begins to dawn on me. Perhaps this is about my reliance on clocks and time and keeping schedules. It's true. Time has been ruling my life for years now. I pack in meeting upon meeting, day after day, as if busyness will prove to me my value and my worth. It's as if I'm competing with myself to do more and more. In reflecting, I also realize when I'm with someone, I'm not giving that person my full attention; I've developed the habit of always glancing at my watch.

"What are you going to do with this?" Craig asks, with his customary kindness and a hint of humor in his voice. I sit with the question for several minutes, silently, before I respond.

"I think this has something to do with time," I finally reply. "But I don't know exactly what it means yet." Impulsively, yet somehow instinctively, I remove the watch from my wrist and toss it on his desk. He laughs and takes off his watch and tosses it next to mine. "I'm in too!" he says.

⁓

That night I crawl under my billowy white down comforter, looking forward to sleep after a day preoccupied with the 3:15 messages. It's a mystery. The book, *Einstein's Dreams* is with me in bed. And because I've been having very interesting dreams lately, I've started keeping a dream journal and going to dream group gatherings once a week. The women in this group are important friends to me: Pam, Gayle, Judy, and Nora. We share something special - a curiosity about life and an interest in finding meaning in our experiences.

The boxes of dream journals I've been carrying around with me are a great reference in finding pieces of inspiration for this work of dream analysis. I've discovered there are many different perspectives on dream interpretation. It's become a rich field of information and study, especially in the emerging field of transpersonal psychology. I've recorded my dreams sporadically over the years, but begin to explore more deeply their possible meanings and symbolism, studying different approaches of interpretation and working with friends in these dream groups.

My friend Nora and I discover we've both utilized the system of dream interpretation advanced by Jeremy Taylor, and we've both been using his tool kit. It resonates with us. For example, he says that all dreams speak a universal language and come in the service of health and wholeness. He also states that only the dreamer can say with any certainty what the meanings of our dreams may be. For us, this certainty comes in the form of a mental "aha!" moment of recognition.

In our dream group, we each take turns sharing a dream. We begin our response to one another with the phrase, "If that were my dream..." and tell one another what the dream might mean to each of us. We ask one another questions like, "What were you feeling when that happened? What were your emotions? Were you frightened? Happy? Angry? Ashamed?" The underlying emotions are as important as the symbols we're exploring.

When other people appear in our dreams, we ask one another, "Name three words that describe that person." Those three words describe aspects of ourselves that we know or need to explore more deeply. They may be aspects that we deny or don't see or want to strengthen.

My friend Gayle has a great habit of writing down the key words she hears from the dream, rather than focusing on the details of the story itself. This makes sense to me since many of my dreams seem to come in disconnected fragments, jumping from one situation to another without logic or connection. Because of her, I've gone back through my journals and underlined words that are interesting and informative. I underline phrases that are repetitive or might have multiple meanings.

I'm quite certain that the way we perceive time limits us. When we're asleep, the past and future constellates in interesting, timeless ways.

I glance over at the nightstand to make sure my journal is next to my bed. I now know I need to write down my dreams the moment I wake before I forget the important details. I have the sense that I'm experiencing a different realm of consciousness in my dream state, and these dreams are leading me to new and undiscovered places in my psyche, instructing me or guiding me through symbols and metaphors. I'm living in the questions now as if I'm living in my own personal sequence of mysteries to be explored and discovered.

While I practice no organized religion any longer in my daily life, I still believe in prayer. It's part of my spiritual practice. Tonight as I relax beneath the covers, I pray to receive a message or guidance from God while I dream. I ask for answers and direction.

6
LOVE

*"We must be willing to let go of
the life we planned, so as to have
the life that is waiting for us."*

Joseph Campbell (1904–1987)

I'm very involved in my community now with the local Chamber of Commerce and the Rotary Club. My career is in high gear. I regularly serve on committees and programs promoting women in business. I'm elected to chair the Downtown Alliance Business Improvement District and serve on the board of the United Way. Through these civic activities, I come to know a remarkable young man who influences my life most profoundly.

I love David the instant I meet him. Our connection might best be described as chemistry or kismet. He's funny, incredibly handsome and playful, and our attraction and connection is immediate. It's honest, heartfelt and obvious to everyone who sees the two of us together. I'm married and he is gay. Our love is simply love, without agendas or expectations -- unconditional and joyful. Our hearts connect. And how he makes me laugh! But because David doesn't feel it's necessary to explain to people that he's gay, and because I don't feel its important either, we're often asked if we're having an affair, which amuses us both enormously!

One day David tells me he's HIV positive. At this time, in the 80's, it's a certain and absolute sentence of death. With the knowledge that his days are numbered and his life will certainly be short-lived, David sells his successful travel business and moves to Hollywood to pursue his unfulfilled dream to be an actor. He has absolute clarity that his short life is going to be lived doing something he's passionate and excited about. He tells me he isn't going to waste another precious minute of his life and turns a deaf ear on those who discourage him by citing the odds of certain failure of beginning the pursuit of acting at his age. His influence on me is profound at this time in my life. I've been in a holding pattern in an unhappy relationship for years, seemingly unable to move on with my life, lacking the motivation to do so. Should we have to wait for death to begin its haunting to make a decision for our own happiness? What if we never get a warning sign about our life's nearing end and our last breath comes before we can grab hold of what we've always wanted for ourselves?

David follows the pursuit of his dream with determination, clear intent, and purpose. While he's living in West Hollywood he begins attending lectures with Marianne Williamson. Her lectures are popular in the gay community at the time. He tells me she is a lifeline in reconnecting him with his own inner sense of spirituality that he's never known as a Mormon and a gay man living in Utah.

One day an envelope with a Hollywood return address from David arrives in the mail. Inside I find a thick blue book printed on thin translucent bible-like paper titled, "A Course in Miracles." The note inside says "Read this. It's my gift to you."

I try to read the book repeatedly because it's a gift from David. "Try" is the operative word here. After a number of unsuccessful starts, it ends up on a bookshelf in my living room. It just doesn't resonate with me, and I feel resistant to the "God" message of the writing. While I feel a profound spiritual calling and connection since my childhood, like many people, I've become cynical of traditional, religious, and dogmatic views. After years of devout Catholic parenting and schooling which included attending mass six days a week, I've simply had enough of organized religion. My ongoing resistance to religion is what causes me to put the book on a shelf.

Until one day, that is, when I'm sitting at the dining room table reading the newspaper and the book falls off the shelf onto the floor. It's the only book that falls, among dozens of other books. I put it back. A few days later it falls off the shelf again. The third time it falls, it has my attention. I tend to think my love for David and the fact that he wanted me to read this book is what prompted me to pick it up again and begin to read. This time is different; it's speaking to me.

I underline a sentence in the Preface:

> *"Its only purpose is to provide a way in which some people will be able to find their own Internal Teacher."*

This one sentence reassures me. It opens my mind and I continue reading. I can relate to the approach of an "internal teacher."

I read the entire book in one sitting, contrary to the book's instructions. I underline sentence after sentence. I note Section VI in Chapter 5, Time and Eternity. *"We have repeatedly said that time is a learning device to be abolished when it is no longer useful."* Here it is again -- a reference to the meaning of time.

I make plans to meet David to see how he's doing and talk about the book. A few weeks later, I fly to California to meet up with him in San Francisco. He takes me to see the Canadian production, Cirque du Soleil, in a tent that holds about 100 people in a parking lot in a sketchy part of the city. Like everything about David, it is magical. We share a room at the Sir Francis Drake Hotel, and that night David opens up to me in an intimate and urgent way that he hasn't done before. He tells me his greatest wish for me is for me to be happy. He knows my marriage isn't good for me. He asks me a very simple and direct question. *"What are you waiting for?"* He asks me this with such sincerity and love!

His frank question reaches in and grabs hold of my heart. I can't shake it because it's coming from him out of absolute love for me, and from someone living day to day with the realization of the pricelessness of each moment of human life.

He returns to L.A. the next day and I have the day to

myself in the city. I walk for hours. I think about David and how he's become an unexpected teacher for me about love and the preciousness of life.

As I sit at a sidewalk cafe on Fisherman's Wharf, relaxing and breathing in the salty air of the bay breeze, I look down at my hands and notice my diamond wedding ring is missing. I know I was wearing it when I left the hotel this morning. Panic sets in. The 2-carat diamond is the most valuable possession I own. I remind myself that my ring has fallen off my finger before, and I always find it. I search inside my purse and the pockets of my jacket. It isn't there. I begin walking back to the hotel, trying to remember, did I turn here? Did I walk past this building? Did I stop in this store? Does this look familiar? And then a calmness and peace settles over me. Is this a sign, I wonder? Is David right? Is it time for me to finally let go of this relationship, this marriage? Is losing my wedding ring a powerful symbolic message?

My mother taught me to believe in the power of prayer. When I was a very young child, I lost a cherished doll I'd been given for Christmas one year. She told me to pray to St. Anthony of Padua, the patron saint of lost things. I did. Afterwards, I found my doll. So I say a prayer to St. Anthony now in homage to her and my childhood.

As I walk back to the hotel something unexplainable and simply unbelievable happens. I glance at a window ledge of an apartment building, and there on the outside window sill, is my diamond wedding ring. I am dumbfounded and stunned. Did someone find it and put it there? Re-reading this in my journal now, I still find it nearly impossible to believe.

I put the ring in my wallet and said a heart-felt thanks to St. Anthony and my mother for any part they may have played in this astonishing turn of events. I also thank David for planting in me the idea of letting go of a relationship that no longer serves me.

The letting go process, the return to love and trust in an unknowable power has been reignited in me. Before heading to the airport, I shop for a writing journal. I pick one with the inscription on the inside cover, a Rumi quote:

> *"Your task is not to seek for love, but merely to seek*
> *and find all the barriers within yourself that you*
> *have built against it."*

Through the process of David's eventual passing from this physical world, I've come to realize the poignancy of the process of death and rebirth. I think about how he was reborn into a new life as an actor. I feel blessed to accompany him and witness his rebirth, realizing his personal dream while facing into the eyes of death. He inspires me to embrace my own process of rebirth and fearlessly walk forward to new possibilities.

7

TRANSITIONS

*"All we have to decide is what to do
with the time that is given to us."*

J.R.R. Tolkien (1892–1973)

I'm about to embark on a journey. It begins when I'm asked to staff a senior executive corporate retreat for my employer, a large multi-state diversified energy company that has recently gone through a merger. They spare no expense in bringing executives of the two newly-merged companies together to begin the process of examining and combining two very historically disparate corporate cultures. The required pre-retreat reading is a book titled *"The Heart Aroused, Poetry and the Preservation of the Soul in Corporate America"* by David Whyte. I snag an extra copy and read the book cover to cover in one sitting.

Whyte is an English poet whose work and philosophy is based on what he describes as "the conversational nature of reality." He acknowledges he grew up with a strong Irish mother who had an imaginative influence on him. With a degree in Marine Zoology, he lived and worked as a naturalist guide in the Galapagos Islands. Love of nature is embedded in his writing and spoken word.

I'm anticipating Whyte's talk as the keynote speaker at the executive retreat. He's one of the few poets bringing perspectives on creativity into the field of organizational development and corporate life. I'm intrigued.

On page 22, coincidentally the floor on which my office is located in the downtown high-rise, he writes:

> *"Work is bounded by time. The soul of a person lies*
> *outside of time and belongs to the unknown, it is the*
> *sacred otherness of existence."*

Again the reference to time strikes a chord in me, re-awakening my curiosity of its meaning once again. The soul lies outside of time? I begin to realize how out of place I'm feeling in my work environment, as if a voice is calling me to step outside this familiar, safe world I've created through work.

I hear my soul say "yes" to this realization. I'm yearning for less structure, fewer restrictions, and a greater sense of creativity. I find myself more and more willing to drop the conventional boundaries imposed by my upbringing and religious training and to reconsider my own desire to be accepted, successful and admired. My creative impulses are calling me.

The author asks a question in his writing. *"Are you leaving your soul in your car in the parking lot when you come to work every day?"* It's a simple yet profound question. Again, I hear my soul answer affirmatively. I'm beginning to feel the need to bring my work life under scrutiny and to re-examine its purpose and meaning. This question begins to live with me.

When I hear David Whyte speak at the retreat, I'm struck by his thoughtful commentary and his effective use of long pauses which allows listeners time to ponder his words and questions. I'm haunted by his thought-provoking presentation. When the student is ready, the teacher shows up. Guess I'm ready.

⁓

It's fall, my favorite time of year, bringing cooler air and the changing colors of the land and leaves. I feel reinvigorated during this season.

My friends Pam, Gayle and Suzanne invite me to take a spiritual pilgrimage with them and Marianne Williamson to visit sacred sites in England, Ireland and Wales. We're to engage in visiting historically significant holy places, spiritual discourse and contemplative practices. My friend David would be delighted that I'm going to meet his muse and inspirator. I'm about to make a connection with one of his favorite teachers and a truly accomplished and powerful woman.

I meet Marianne in the passenger waiting area outside

the check-in gate at JFK airport. After the flight to London's Heathrow airport, we board the charter bus to our hotel and then settle into our rooms. Marianne refers to us as a group of "pilgrims." We're taking a journey to sacred places for spiritual reflection. Later in the day, we meet downstairs and circle our chairs to introduce ourselves to one another. When it's my turn, out of a perverse habit I've developed of leading with my identity as it's tied to my job, I begin, "I work for the Power Company." Without hesitation and embodied in her powerful voice and cryptic, delightful humor, Marianne replies forcefully, "So do I!" We laugh together. I feel a mighty connection. Thus begins a relationship with an exceptional female mentor and teacher for me.

Since beginning this phase of my career in the 70's, I've been working for an electrical utility where 90% of the workforce are male engineers, accountants and linemen. There are few women in the workplace and most of them are in secretarial and support roles.

The context for this period of time is helpful to understand. When I began working in the early 70's, there was no maternity leave, let alone family leave. Child care was difficult to find. This was before the "business" of child care began. Living in Utah, I observed that the Mormon Church frowned on women members working outside the home. This meant there were very few professional women in my place of work. You could call it a female professional work desert of sorts.

Women like me, who were pursuing professional careers, were often seen as objects of curiosity (and other kinds of objects as well, #metoo). The majority of jobs available to women were clerical in nature. I started my career in the type pool. It wasn't long before I was promoted to an Executive Assistant to a vice president. This guy liked to put his dirty dishes in his outbox for me to carry to the kitchen after eating lunch at his desk every day. Surprised and offended, in an act of defiance I lifted up the dirty dishes, took the paperwork out from under them, and put them back in his outbox without saying a word. It wasn't long before his wife paid a visit to the office and had the hubris to reprimand me, asserting my role was to be his "office wife."

Upon meeting Marianne, I said to myself, "Now here's a powerful, intellectual, spiritual woman with a wicked sense of humor that I can relate to!" No more office wife for me!

Our time together on the "pilgrimage" begins early every morning over continental breakfast and a lecture on the sacred sites we will be visiting. During the day, we sit in contemplative practice and engage in prayer along the route to the different historical locations. We listen to lectures on history and spirituality, followed every evening by a closing ceremony before bedtime. We visit earthen henges and cathedrals, Glastonbury Tor, Stonehenge and many of the historically valuable sites in England and Ireland.

In the windy, small farm-laden area of Ireland, ancient stone walls and earthen mounds peek out from green hills to the observant eye. This part of the Emerald Isle is magical. Our bus driver pulls over one morning so we can snap photos of a crop circle that has enchantingly appeared. I'm fascinated with the seemingly random "warning" signs for motorists where "ley lines" cross the roads in rural areas of Ireland. I discovered the term "ley lines" has been used to describe various geographic alignments of the world's ancient megaliths and monuments. I make notes in my travel journal.

After several days, we board a ferry from Ireland to Wales and meet up with another chartered bus for our drive to the English county of Somerset. One morning we visit Glastonbury

Tor and the famous landmark of St. Michael's Tower, a place that holds a long religious history and huge spiritual significance for many people. It contains evidence of Pagan and early Christian settlement.

While at Glastonbury Tor, we are greeted by John Michell, an author and expert on ancient knowledge. He shares complex scientific and philosophical ideas with us. He's humble and unassuming in both speech and demeanor. Educated at Trinity College in Cambridge, he served in the Royal Navy and later served as a Russian interpreter in civil service. His published works include views on sacred geometry and largely ignored works of ancient wisdom. I feel that I'm in the presence of a consummate teacher as he sits patiently, answering our many questions.

At each site, we begin with meditation led by Marianne, followed by a lecture and discussions. The group begins to develop an intimate and authentic affinity with one another. I feel a shift at a cellular level in my body, my mind and my soul. I feel a congruity with something larger than myself - a collective consciousness that goes back through history and time, woven together in spiritual practice and ancient rituals, bound together in this moment with fellow travelers. I also feel a deep personal connection to this place; this is the land of my mother's ancestors. My grandmother's family roots can be traced to Ireland and Scotland -- the Kennedys and the Armstrongs.

I close my eyes one night and reflect on my friend David. I convey my thanks to him for his friendship and his service to me by challenging my thinking and demanding that I live a happier life.

8
GIFT

"I can give many things even before you know you want them, but when you know, it's quicker and more joyful."

Mother Meera

In this dream, I'm walking around inside a gift shop. The place appears to be deserted. I browse around, taking in the bookshelves lined with stacks of books, the art on the walls and the jewelry in the glass display cases. The colors and hues are rich, deep and saturated, yet the lighting is dim. Out of the corner of my eye, I detect a movement and notice a beautiful, serene young Indian woman in a turquoise blue sari, watching me quietly from behind the counter.

Her warm and inviting blackish-brown eyes kindly beckon me to come closer. I lean forward to get a better look and notice the red colored dot, a bindi, between the woman's eyebrows. "Hello, my name is Mother Meera," she says softly, extending her hand to me. I lean in and look at her outstretched hand. A brilliant light emanates from her small, brown open palm. The light saturates me and I'm instantly filled with incredible joy and peace. My body, my ego, and my personality dissolve. I am formless, faceless, and have the sensation of dissolving into an essence of pure, radiant and blissful love and warmth.

When morning comes, I awaken to bright, warm sunlight shining on my face from the window above my bed. I'm still infused with the feeling of pure love and peace from my dream. I'm both delighted and bewildered at the same time.

Reaching for my dream journal beside the bed, I begin to write, wondering how to spell her name. Mirror? Mira? Meera? Myra?

Is the gift shop symbolic? Am I being given a gift through the dream, I wonder?

It's Saturday morning and I get dressed to meet my dream group friends for breakfast at the Oasis restaurant in the Golden Braid bookstore. This is our weekend ritual. We've been friends for some time, having shared many experiences together- marriages, divorces, lovers, challenges in life, much joy and a great deal of mischief. My friendships with these women are important. We stand with one another in deep compassion, without judgment and with loving support. We're also radically honest.

I believe in shared sisterhood. We look out for one another, we protect each other. This sisterhood extends into my professional life as well, having been honored with the Chamber of Commerce Pathfinder Award for assisting and mentoring other women. Sisterhood is a deeply held value in my life.

I park my car in the lot behind the bookstore and as I reach for the handle on the back door, I notice a sign that reads, "Hang out in good company…" it begins. "The Dalai Lama, Deepak Chopra, Marianne Williamson, Ram Dass, Mother Meera." I stare in disbelief. Oh my God. The woman from my dream is real!

In the astonishing turn of events of the moment, I disregard the friends waiting for me in the restaurant, and stride deliberately into the bookstore. The sales clerk and I have become friends over the years and I ask if he knows of Mother Meera. Nodding, he leads me down an aisle to a section on world religions and pulls a small paperback book off the shelf. Staring back at me from the cover is a photograph of the beautiful young woman from my dream. I look up at him in wide-eyed wonder.

I don't understand what's been happening to me for some time now. First, the clocks stopping, then the book on my desk, and now the dream, validated by another book. It's extraordinary. I'm not prepared nor equipped with how to understand or interpret this. I hurry into the next room to find my friends in the restaurant, tucking two books and the receipt inside my purse.

We meet every weekend for breakfast here. We've been doing this for several years. Their eyes sparkle and dance with excitement as I tell them about the clocks, the dream and the books. Imaginations and theories run wild while we share our breakfast and coffee. Today I don't linger with them like I normally would. I'm excited to get home to explore Mother Meera's book, *"Answers, Part I."*

I read about Mother Meera's life and work in the world, and her belief about her calling, which is to heal the planet, particularly Germany, after the brutal political Nazi regime. She posits that this kind of trauma is held not only in the physical world, but culturally and personally for generations. I'm intrigued by her spiritual calling which was exhibited and recognized when she was a young girl in India by her uncle, who mentored and supported her. Meera's artwork reminds me of my own creative side and I begin to search in my closets for my sketchbooks. It's been a while since I've used one, and I find them in storage bins in my basement. I select one. Holding it is familiar, like holding a family member I haven't seen in a while. I flip through the pages, remembering this abandoned creative side of myself.

At the back of Mother Meera's book is a telephone number for her house in Germany where she holds "darshan" with visitors. I feel I must follow up on this and that I must call. Is it intuition? Or is it an innate sense of knowing? Calculating the time zone difference, I pick up the phone and punch in the numbers.

A male voice answers, "Mother Meera's house." Surprised to hear an actual voice and not a recording, I explain why I'm calling and describe the dream and the sign at the bookstore.

I surely must sound like a nut case to the man on the other end of the line. After listening to me ramble, he suggests I should visit Meera in Germany and sit with her in darshan. Darshan? I wonder, what's that? He recommends I stay for two weeks. I hear myself agree. I don't even question it, and then I dial a friend in the travel business and begin making air and hotel reservations. I research "darshan" and discover that in Hinduism, it refers to the beholding of a deity, revered person or sacred object. The experience is considered to be reciprocal and results in the human observer receiving a blessing.

The next day at my office I tell Craig about the dream and my travel plans, and he smiles and gives me a thumbs-up. "Good for you," he says.

I'm reminded of thoughts from Henry David Thoreau.

"If you find yourself suddenly infused with an experience you can't explain, you should be aware that you're not alone."

Thoreau reminds us that all awakenings are woven into great worldly traditions.

Two weeks later the plane touches down on the runway at Frankfurt airport. I look out the small cabin window at gray skies and wake the sleeping passenger next to me, my friend Suzanne. We've been traveling companions before on our pilgrimage to Ireland and England. Her enthusiasm about the messages and the dream unfolding has drawn her into this adventure with me. It feels gratifying to have her support and service as my witness to this unfolding mystery and the recent improbable events.

I've carried with me several books to read on the flight, Jack Kornfield's *"A Path with Heart"* and Marianne Williamson's *"A Return to Love."* Books are constant companions.

I'm reminded of something Martin Luther King, Jr. said - that faith is taking the first step, even when you don't see the whole staircase. I recall the recurring theme of staircases in my dream journals and that for me, stairs convey progress and moving backward or forward in my life. Going up the stairs suggests forward progress while going down the stairs represents reflecting back or going inside and doing inner work.

This concept seems particularly apt in my present situation. It's a reassuring message as I follow this internal staircase of sorts, into the next phase of my journey. But I wonder, am I going up the stairs, or down them? Or both?

9
JOURNEY

"One thing about trains, it doesn't matter where they're going, what matters is deciding to get on."

Conductor, *The Polar Express*

I can't remember the last time I was on a train and I'm intoxicated with this adventure. What a joy it will be to spend time looking out the window, watching the countryside roll by with the lull of gentle rocking back and forth along the way.

After arriving at the Frankfurt Airport, Suzanne and I find our bags and make our way outside. Many taxis are lined up for arriving passengers. We stand at the end of the queue to grab a cab across town to the train station. A jet-lag induced blur has taken hold of me and before I realize it, I'm standing on the platform of the train station facing a black, ancient-looking machine. Zombie-like, we board. The conductor checks each passenger's ticket and directs us to the first car, immediately behind the engine. I'm struck by the contrast of this old black coal-fired train and the sleek, modern aluminum express train on the track across from us. Is this symbolic? This causes me to feel as though I'm traveling back in time.

A spiritual teacher once told me that when we practice meditation and heal, we not only heal ourselves, but that we heal our ancestors back seven generations. I imagine this as I look at these two trains; one old, one new.

The train slowly works its way toward the mountains and our final destination, dropping passenger cars along the way in small villages. I understand now why we've been directed to the front car by the conductor. We're going to be the last stop; only the engine and this car will make the final climb to the small village of Limburg. I'm looking forward to exploring the historic town, originally built in the 7ᵗʰ century with many homes 800 years old and beautifully restored.

Along the slow and final stretch of the route, the gentle rocking of the train and squeals of steel rails lull me to sleep. I'm awakened by the gentle hand of an attendant shaking my shoulder. Startled, I reach over to wake Suzanne. I don't know how long the train's been stopped or how long we've been asleep. I realize I've been dreaming again. I reach for my journal to capture the details before I forget them. Then I step outside into the sunshine and brisk air for the final leg of the trip to Thalheim where Mother Meera lives.

At last we reach the village. This medieval town is well-preserved with interesting half-timbered houses, some dating back to the 13th century. The white houses with their red and black framework offer a unique and pleasant sight upon our arrival. A cathedral that resembles a candy-embellished gingerbread house greets my eyes.

When we arrive at our lodging, a somber plump German woman checks us in and hands us a room key with large wooden attachments with a room number. Tersely, she instructs us to leave the key at the front desk when we go out. Turning back, I remember to ask for directions to Mother Meera's house. Her demeanor noticeably changes then. She frowns and replies something unintelligible in a deep German accent. She's intentionally avoiding eye contact with me when I ask her questions. I learn later from some of the regular visitors to darshan that many of the older residents in the village resent the intrusion of what they consider new-age spiritual pilgrims and devotees to Mother Meera.

I climb a narrow, creaky flight of stairs to my room on the third floor, dragging my huge over-packed suitcase loudly up the wood steps. The room is narrow with two twin beds and a small refrigerator at one end, stocked with drinks and mini bottles of Jagermeister, a German liqueur. I help myself to a mini bottle and the dark, bitter drink tastes surprisingly good. I lay on the bed and finally relax as it hits my bloodstream. I'm physically tired, yet my mind is restless and anxious.

Since the day in which time stopped at 3:15, I've been

following a trail of synchronicities in waking and sleep time. I trust my hunches a little bit more, and following one, I look inside the dresser and find a bible. I flip through chapters and pages and pause on the book of Ecclesiastes, verse 3:15. It's in German. I make a note to myself to follow up on this.

Lying on the bed in my hotel room in Thalheim, the Jagermeister and jet lag kick in at last. I drift off and dream. Suddenly awakened by the sound of voices in the hallway, I remember I'm in Germany. I've noticed the nature of my dreams has changed since I decided to take this trip. Instead of being narrative in nature, they've become visual with symbols and images, like pictograms. I take a moment to draw them in my journal and make notes about the way I feel when I wake. The emotions and feelings I experience in the dreams seem as important as the content, maybe even more so now.

Later, when I return home, I refer to the Saint Joseph New Catholic Edition, Ecclesiastes 3:15.

> *"There is an appointed time for everything and a time for every purpose under heaven."* It continues, *"What now is, has already been; what is to be, already is."*

Curious. Yes, it seems to confirm that whatever this message is, once again, it must have something to do with time. But what exactly does that passage mean? Is the message one of religion or science? I notice my dichotomous thinking just now. Does it have to be one or the other, or could it be both?

10
DARSHAN

"We are asleep with compasses in our hands."

W. K. Merwin

I look for the written instructions from Mother Meera's staff and re-read them. After arriving in Thalheim, we're told to meet at the Town Hall parking lot to be escorted to Meera's house. The travelers gathering this afternoon reflect a variety of ages and nationalities. There are about 30 people. A tall blonde German man introduces himself as Andrew. After brief introductions and pleasantries, Suzanne and I are invited to the front of the line of visitors because we have traveled the longest distance and this is our first time to darshan. We exchange smiles with one another. I'm happy and hyped-up to finally be here.

In a group, we walk across the street through a residential neighborhood comprised of small simple homes on narrow streets. We're asked to line up outside her house by the back door before we're instructed to enter silently in a single-file line.

Chairs are carefully arranged with typical German-style precision on both sides of the room, theatre style. An empty chair is centered in the space with a red carpet leading up to it from the main entryway, facing a staircase in the hallway. Cushions are arranged on the floor in front of the chairs. Not knowing quite what to expect, and feeling somewhat uncertain about what's going to happen next, I take a place in the second row of chairs to wait and watch.

As I'm sitting here, I remember my uncle Richard telling me about one of our German ancestors, Christianus Reineccius, a Saxon theologian from the 18th Century. He described him as a linguist and prolific writer. As Rector of the Weissenfels Academy he was commissioned to translate the bible into four languages – Hebrew, Greek, Latin and German. And it occurs to me that the bible in my hotel room which I picked up when I arrived is most likely a result of his work in the 1700's. Suddenly I'm intrigued by the intimacy I feel from this personal connection to a paternal ancestor who lived centuries before my existence.

I think of my father, Robert, stationed somewhere in Germany during World War II. The Limburg Airfield was built by the Luftwaffe in 1944 to protect the Limburg railroad. It was later captured by American forces and was also the location of the first American wartime radio broadcast east of the Rhine River. My father was trained and deployed to build and operate radios during the war. Were they used for these broadcasts? I have dozens of letters he wrote to his mother in Minnesota during the war, which have given me insight into the man he was before I was born. The humility and respect he demonstrated for his mother in his hand-written letters is striking. Is it mere coincidence that I've been summoned here by this stranger who lives in Germany named Mother Meera?

I'm brought back to the moment when the mystery woman from the dream enters the room and is seated in the chair. It's amazing that I've come all this way to my father's ancestral land, summoned by a dream, and I'm now in her presence. She looks exactly as she appeared in my dream! The crowded room is reverent in its silence. The swishing of her sari is the only sound to be heard. After several minutes, following a nod from her assistant, people line up to kneel before her and she places her hands on each person's head for a few moments. When she's finished, she rests her hands in her lap and stares deeply into each person's eyes. I'm struck by the fact that her face remains absolutely expressionless during these interactions. I was expecting something different, like the warm face and engaged eyes that I experienced in my dream.

Watching and waiting until everyone has knelt before her, I anxiously take my turn. Kneeling, with my head bowed, I feel her place her hands on my head. Her fingers are firm and strong and she adjusts them slightly, and then holds them firmly in place for several seconds before releasing her grip. Mimicking the behavior of those who've gone before me, I sit back on my heels. As I look up into her eyes, I see the first reaction of the evening on her face, which registers surprise through widened eyes. Then she looks through me for several seconds and lowers her gaze. I return to my chair with the sense of being stared at and look up to see Meera's assistant, Adelakshmi, examining me.

Outside in the crisp mountain air, Suzanne exclaims, "She recognized you!" So it wasn't only me who felt that; Suzanne saw the surprise and recognition on her face as well, just like Meera's assistant did. This affirms it was right for me to come here, even though I don't know why and I still have many questions. Who is this woman? What is an Indian hindu woman doing in Germany? Why am I here? What am I supposed to do with this?

Every day we walk to Meera's home to sit in darshan with other pilgrims from around the world. We meditate collectively and it seems to be a grounding, peaceful, and calm way of being in Germany, once the epicenter of war and death.

Sunday morning arrives and I say goodbye as Suzanne heads home to Salt Lake City. Andrew drives me to another hotel for my second week of stay.

Meera's assistants have taken me under their wing and have arranged a room at another hotel that is friendlier to her followers and her work. "You're the only guest for the next two nights," the hotel owner explains. "There is another American arriving on Wednesday. His name is John. He visits twice a year." My room is bright, clean and comfortable, yet sparsely furnished. I decide to take a shower and write about my experience here. Since darshan takes place in the late afternoon, during the days I take long walks through the village and surrounding hillsides.

Thalheim is in the Ore Mountains in Saxony. It's an industrial town with a 16ᵗʰ century mill, old mining tunnels and is distinctly German and conservative. There's also a notable grayness here, even when the sun is out. It's as though the pain and suffering of war still lingers in the DNA of the countryside and seems haunted by the ghosts of those who lost their lives here.

Each night my dreams continue. I draw and sleep, dream and draw. During the day, I hike the forests and the hillsides carrying my backpack with my journal and sketchbook.

My dreams are now wild and disturbing, filled with demonic forces, darkness and disturbing events. Nightmares wake me often during the night and I feel terrified and frightened. There's a recurring theme of being chased and running from danger. There's a tension with these opposites I'm experiencing- the contrasting forces of peaceful quiet contemplation in waking life battling the dark vexing dream states that paralyze me in my sleep. Is this a reflection of my internal struggle of dark versus light? My personal struggle between my creative and professional life? My father's struggle between love of his ancestral German roots and engagement in WWII against the Germans?

I've begun to study the work of Carl Gustav Jung, the Swiss psychiatrist and psychoanalyst. My Swiss/German paternal grandparents both had the given name of Gustav. Another coincidence perhaps. Jung suggests that dreams reveal both the personal and collective unconscious. He also proposes that archetypes such as the anima, the shadow and the animus are often represented in figures in dreams. I continue to explore the possible meanings of these frightening figures and experiences from my dreams. It's a riddle for me.

I'm also drawn to the research of dreams by Calvin Hall, who proposed that dreams are part of our cognitive process. It's helpful to look for themes and patterns by reviewing many of my past dreams in my dream journals. I like his approach that the ultimate goal is to understand the dreamer, not the dream; that dreams are like windows into the subconscious of the dreamer.

One evening I'm awakened from a deep sleep to the sound of a loud male American voice coming from the room across the hall. This must be the guest named John, the man the owner mentioned when I arrived. I meet him at breakfast the next morning in the hotel's dining room. I like him instantly with his freckles, red hair and easy, comfortable friendliness. He's encyclopedic with his knowledge and has spent time with spiritual teachers across the globe. We discover we have many common interests. It surprises me to learn he's a golf pro at an exclusive country club in New York during summers and earns enough money to travel the rest of the year. He has apartments in India and Thailand, he tells me. What a life, I think, and such a stark contrast with my corporate 50-hour work week.

Admittedly, I feel envious of his lifestyle. That is the kind of life I'd love to live. How did I get trapped in a corporate merry-go-round when spirituality, art and adventure are the passions that fuel me, I wonder.

John asks me why I'm here and I tell him about the dream of Mother Meera and then the flyer on the back door of the bookstore, giving credence to her actual existence. I share my spiritual journey and the teachers I've met and the books I'm reading. He shares his with me. He is a kindred spirit for certain.

John gives me a book, *The Mother*, by Sri Aurobindo, and a laminated photograph of his spiritual collaborator known simply as "The Mother." I'm touched by his kindness and his generosity. I learn Sri Aurobindo is best known for his philosophy on human evolution and Integral Yoga. He was also a political activist, a mystic and a spiritual leader. I make a note in my journal to explore this further and learn more about him and his work with his protege, known simply as The Mother.

John and I hang out together for the remainder of my stay in Germany. John seems to understand what's happening to me and doesn't find my experiences to be weird or strange in the slightest. As the last night of darshan approaches, I feel myself becoming anxious, because I still don't have answers about the dream of Mother Meera or why she appeared to me. I mention this to Andrew, one of her assistants, and he tells me she expects people to ask her for something so she can grant their wishes.

I walk to Meera's house for my final day of darshan and Adelakshmi meets me at the door. It seems she's been waiting for me. She directs me to sit on the back staircase which is unexpected. I'm not sure why I've been relegated to the back staircase. From here I won't be able to see Meera in the main room. I'm disappointed at first but then I find the solitude of the staircase more peaceful and calming than the room packed with people and the inherent distractions of the parade of strangers lining up and kneeling to receive darshan.

While I'm thinking about my latest series of dreams, I'm brought back to the present moment when I hear the familiar swish of Meera's sari behind me and look up the staircase to meet her piercing gaze. My smile is automatic. Her smiling response is, too. It's the first time I've seen her smile since I've come to visit, and then she passes by, walking through the door into the large room. I wonder if this was the purpose of Adelakshmi seating me on the staircase; that I might have this personal encounter? I wait for the signal from her helpers that it's my turn to enter the main room, remembering the frightening dreams this past week. And then - in an instant, I know what it is I want to ask of her. It's protection. I want protection; protection from seemingly dangerous men who've been haunting me in my adult life and my dream life.

I relax now, feeling relieved and certain, and close my eyes. At that moment, her face instantly appears in my mind's eye and I hear her answer me silently and immediately, "It is so."

I kneel in front of her one last time, feeling like a weight has been lifted off my shoulders. I somehow know that now I'm protected, and I'm grateful and ready to return home. My visit feels complete.

On the return flight from Frankfurt to JFK, I re-read the book left on the corner of my desk a few weeks ago. An idea about time captures my interest. It puts forth the notion that time is a circle bending back on itself in which the world repeats itself over and over again. I reach for my journal to find the quote from Ecclesiastes, 3:15.

> "There's an appointed time for everything and a
> time for every purpose under heaven."

I'm thinking about the mystery of time and our relationships and how a look into the eyes of a seeming complete stranger can sometimes be met with instant knowing, recognition, and trust. I think about the connections I've made with my paternal ancestors on this trip to Germany- my father, my grandfather, back seven generations to Christianus Reineccius. I wonder if we've known each other before, or if, perhaps, someone from the past is looking through my eyes and speaking to me through my thoughts. In healing ourselves, I wonder, do we heal these others?

11

PROTECTION

"The best protection any woman can have is courage."

Elizabeth Cady Stanton (1815–1902)

I've been thinking about my request for protection since returning home from Germany. It seems especially relevant at this particular period of my life.

I graduated from high school when I was 17 years old and over the next 20 years, life became progressively more challenging and complicated. I began working full time and going to school at night. I withdrew from my family and found myself drawn into a difficult and vexing relationship with an older man I worked for. I was a painfully shy, introverted, naive girl. I didn't have the wisdom or worldly experience necessary to deal with the attention and advances of this confident, assertive man. I had been protected and shielded from much of the outside world by my loving parents throughout my childhood. I was sheltered by them.

My memories about this era of my life play in slow motion and are painful while I scrutinize what happened to me. When I met the man who was to become my future husband, I was just out of high school, interviewing for a summer job. I was recommended to him by one of the nuns who taught me at St. Mary's.

During the interview, I was drawn to this man's intellect and world view. He hired me and showered me with personal attention, which I hadn't known as a child from a large family. I was raised to be an accommodating caregiver. This was what my parents valued in me and rewarded me for- taking care of others first, before myself.

As my new employer spoke about his life experiences, I became fascinated with the idea of world travel and romanticized unseen places greater than that of my protective childhood bubble. The seeds of my desire to experience and see the world were fostered by his stories. He was a superb story teller.

I see clearly now in hindsight how he was drawn to the

beauty of my innocence and vulnerability, and in contrast, I see how I was drawn to his confidence, experience and worldview.

We eloped when I was 25 and he was 65. My parents were absolutely devastated by this. I was disowned for five years. It broke my heart.

My father was my first love and our connection was incredibly special when I was a young girl. Our relationship changed when I entered adolescence and womanhood. He put up a barrier. I couldn't understand what I'd done or why I was being treated differently by him. I sensed an invisible wall between us.

Now I understand. As many women who've had a close relationship with their fathers know, this change from being daddy's little girl to becoming a teenager is a confusing time with the sudden onslaught of hormones changing us physically and emotionally. I believe we subconsciously attempt to replace this important closeness with our fathers with another father figure. I see now that I did that.

Without comprehending what I was doing at the time, I replaced my father with another father figure. Our first few years of marriage were great. We built a beautiful new home and traveled to places on our bucket lists. His love for our daughter was joyful to share.

But life wasn't all roses. Our May/December relationship was the subject of much gossip and mockery. People were cruel. Old friends fell away. I experienced a loneliness I hadn't known before. We had golden times together as a family, yet socially we didn't fit in anywhere.

In the beginning of our marriage, my husband showered me with adoration and praise. He gave me accolades for my talent and creativity. He constantly told me I was beautiful and I genuinely felt appreciated. I was content.

The unraveling began slowly with him telling me how to dress, what to eat, and how to wear my hair. One night as we were getting ready to leave the house for an event, he looked me over and told me to go back to my room and change my clothes. Obedient and compliant, I did as he commanded. I see now that I had become one of his possessions.

His behavior progressively worsened. After closing his business and retiring, he stayed home all day. I'd return from work to find him still in his pajamas, sitting at the kitchen table asking, "What are you fixing for me for dinner?"

Then began the bouts of depression, anger and rage. He became paranoid. He'd misplace things around the house and accuse me of hiding them from him. He wouldn't change his clothes or shower. He withdrew into a world of his own, and our connection was lost. The signs of dementia came on slowly, though at the time, I didn't know what dementia was. He refused therapy for PTSD, holding onto the belief that as a survivor of World War II, he should "tough it out." The combination of his symptoms of dementia and PTSD became increasingly toxic and he started to become physically violent.

It took enormous energy to keep up a positive and cheerful front when my internal world was tethered in darkness. My dark night of the soul experience remained solidly private and unexpressed. I was stoic.

As my career advanced, I felt renewed purpose and fulfillment in my professional life. I kept my personal tragedy hidden from the people around me.

I think about the authentic realization of love I discovered when my daughter was born. This profound love for my daughter, and my sense of responsibility as a parent, was a touchstone for me.

The threat of my husband's unpredictable outbursts of

violence eventually caused me to realize I couldn't stand for it anymore. I couldn't allow our daughter to grow up thinking this is what marriage is supposed to be like. How did I gain the courage and motivation to move on? The love and support of my friend David planted the seed of the thought for me to realize I wanted, and deserved, to be happy and to feel alive once again. I hoped that by moving on, I would be a visible demonstration of the importance of having courage, taking risks, and making changes in the face of a difficult challenge.

It took me many years to acquire the personal power, the will, and the courage to walk away from my marriage. I had come to the realization that at a fundamental and prime soul level, my spirit was dying. There were many signals along the way that I should have paid closer attention to, like withdrawal from my family and friends, as well as a prolonged period of depression. I slept a lot. I stopped taking care of myself and I wasn't excited about life anymore. I traveled for work more than needed to avoid being at home. I spent money on things I didn't need as a distraction from my circumstances. I knew I had to make a change in my life in order to feel alive again.

When did it end? What did it take? How did I gain the courage and motivation to move on?

It happened on a seemingly ordinary day. I simply got ready for work earlier than usual while he and our daughter slept. I loaded my car with my clothes and basic necessities. I called in sick to work. I took the day to find and rent an apartment in a secure building. There was nothing I could do to fix the brokenness. I'd grown up. I no longer needed a parent; I wanted a partner.

I couldn't foresee the implications of what the disruption that my leaving would create. For my daughter, she was losing her idyllic childhood. She was caught in between two people she loved. She was conflicted and angry. She blamed me. I know this was a very difficult time in her life. She started having trouble at school. Her teacher called Child Protective Services and they sent a social worker to my new home as well as his, for a "home visit."

Fortunately, not too many years later, as a young woman, she began to understand. I came to realize this the day she asked me why it took so long for me to wake up and leave.

After she turned sixteen and had her driver's license and a car, she drove herself to the YWCA's Women's Shelter to volunteer as a receptionist. She told me she was able to identify the women who were there to change their lives for good and make a serious effort to step forward, and those who would likely remain stuck in the cycle of abuse, domestic violence and victimization. It was immensely gratifying to witness how she turned a difficult life lesson into compassion and service to others. It was incredible for me to witness her own self-realization of her innate leadership ability.

We learned together then. We learned about the insidious nature of PTSD and senile dementia, and we reconciled many of the darker things we'd been through together. Out of this came deep compassion for the suffering and experiences of others facing childhood trauma, disrupted family life, feelings of isolation and loneliness, as well as those suffering from dementia and PTSD. There is comfort and solace in knowing that we are not alone in these experiences.

Now looking back, I know why I asked for protection from Mother Meera in darshan. While my need for protection didn't happen overnight, it can be best illustrated by an incident that occurred a year after I moved out of our house and my marriage.

I woke up during the night to find my estranged husband standing over my bed, watching me. It had become a habit of his during our marriage. Waking up to someone standing over your bed watching you in the dark of night is an alarming emotional experience, even if it is someone you know. And having that happen after I'd moved out and was living in my own home was terrifying. I pretended to be asleep and didn't move until I heard him leave.

I found out later that he'd made a copy of my daughter's house key without her knowledge. The following morning I changed the locks and installed deadbolts and hung bells above all the doors. I kept the blinds closed at all times. I went to the animal shelter and adopted a dog.

This fear of being watched and followed stayed with me. I discovered I'd been unknowingly photographed by him with my friends and that he had copied the license plates of cars in my driveway. He slashed the tires and shattered my car windows, making off with my journals and day planner. He stole mail from the mailbox on my front porch. All of this added to my mental and emotional wounds and fear, and my feelings of powerlessness. It became cumulative and toxic.

Is this why this unhealed part of me came forward through dark dreams and nightmares during my time in Germany? It's likely. I understand now that I was being presented with an opportunity to seek divine intervention and protection. Is this why Mother Meera introduced herself to me? Was this the calling of the dream? Was this the "gift" she was giving me in her appearance in the "gift shop" dream?

And is it possible that this woman who is referred to as "Mother" symbolizes my Higher Self or the Divine Feminine energy, awakening the scared and frightened child to come forward and be healed? Did she appear in order to help me transition from childhood into adulthood? Is this me being empowered to heal these wounds for myself, so many years later?

It's an interesting consideration that this happened in Germany, at the ancestral roots of my paternal genetic DNA, as if my ancestors were beckoning me home to assist me in the beginning of the healing process. It's also interesting that my husband's PTSD began in Germany during World War II. In healing ourselves, do we heal those unhealed parts of our ancestors and other family members too, I wonder?

Perhaps like the archetype Psyche from Greek mythology, the Goddess of the Soul, who traveled to the underworld, it is possible through the intervention of a greater power that we can be healed and reborn in love and life. And only through our own healing do we develop the compassion and capacity to be with others in their suffering.

The power of the heroine's journey described by Jean Shinoda Bolen is illustrated by the story of Psyche through the "underworld" of her inner darkness. In this mythological story, Psyche, a beautiful maiden, personifies the human soul. Psyche was the most beautiful girl on earth, but she was sad and lonely; always admired by never really loved. How true this felt for me. She symbolizes the soul purified by passions and misfortunes and who, through overcoming her misfortunes, is prepared to enjoy eternal happiness. This has been my journey. Whatever the circumstances that surround us, we invariably draw the relationships and teachers in our life for the advancement of our souls.

I'm now able to find peace in the notion that I drew this man into my life so that I might learn important life lessons for the growth of my soul. Lessons like the establishment of my boundaries and my will, the trust in my own inner knowing, compassion, and forgiveness, as well as my own unique and authentic beauty and power.

I continue to listen and learn to recognize a guiding force and divine intervention through dreams, synchronicities and meaningful coincidences. I'm learning to pay attention to unexpected inner voices and synchronicities when they appear. I pride myself that I'm a risk taker and that I'm surrendering to a radical trust in the Universe/God/Higher Power- that invisible force that's present in our lives. By this protection and through this strength I'm able to lead a more purposeful, compassionate, and courageous life today. And I'm daring myself to be vulnerable once again.

12

HOME

"If you experience synchronicities and coincidences, these are anonymous messages coming from God."

Deepak Chopra

I've moved many times in life, having lived in roughly 30 apartments and homes from Minnesota to California, Colorado, Utah and Illinois, and finally back home to stay in Colorado. Some of these moves were the result of my father's employment, and many of them were of my own choosing.

I've learned that home is ultimately not about a place to live but about the people with whom we feel we are most fully alive. Home is about love, relationship with surroundings, a sense of community and belonging. Aren't we all searching for home?

When we inhabit our authentic and vulnerable self, we are home. The search then is internal, not external. This is where true belonging begins- in self-acceptance. There exists in this self-acceptance a sense of belonging. You hear what you're meant to hear. You internalize what is meant for you, just for you. Each of us has the capacity to know, truly know, that at our center lies something right and good. I return home to myself when I rediscover what is right and good through artistic and spiritual exploration. Through courage and determination I find my voice as well an authentic realization of what home truly means.

—

Re-entry to a daily routine after international travel is always a challenging experience. This time it seems returning from Germany it's especially so. On one hand, I've been in an inward-focused introspective place of spiritual renewal. And on the other hand, I find myself returning to a fast-paced, demanding corporate life driven by external forces.

I arrive earlier than usual at my office today to have some quiet time before the chaos of catching up from weeks absorbed in meditation and self-examination.

Rain is hitting the thick panes of glass, leaving snail trails mimicking tears. The sound is hypnotic. I notice the pile of mail and the stack of phone messages on my desk. Pausing, I take a few deep breaths.

When did my job become my life, I ask myself somewhat sadly. It's 7 am on Monday morning when the phone on my desk rings. The sound irritates me and the disruption of my planned quiet time feels intrusive. Who calls at 7am on a Monday morning anyway?!! This incessant voice inside my head says, "Maybe it's God calling." So after the seventh ring I reluctantly pick up the receiver. Ron, from Helper, Utah is on the other end of the line.

Forgoing any pleasantries on his part, he jumps right in and tells me he's been trying to reach me for weeks. There's a sense of urgency in his voice bordering just this side of panic and manic. He insists he needs to see me and says he'll drive to Salt Lake City. I agree to meet him the next day. After I hang up, I check my leather Franklin Day Planner and see the conflict. Damn. This means I have to give up my tickets for a concert tomorrow night that I've been looking forward to for months.

———

I haven't seen or talked to Ron for several years. The sound of his voice takes me back in time, flashing back four years to a drive home from Moab with my bicycle on top of the car. On the front seat is a package; a birthday gift I forgot to mail before leaving home. The highway sign alerts me that I'm approaching the town of Helper and I remember a TV news story about the Post Office closing in this small historic railroad town. A group of local residents squatted on the railroad tracks to block the coal cars from the mines to protest the closure of their historic post office, which like many small towns, is a community gathering place, where you run into your neighbors. The story made the national news.

I follow the signs directing me to the downtown district. Suddenly, I feel I've been transported back in time. A 30's-era diner sits on the corner of Main Street across from the historic train depot. Now time moves fast-forward, but seemingly in real time, I have a lucid vision of this town transformed into an artists' community, with painters and sculptors working behind street-front windows in their studios and galleries. I blink and try to shake it off- but the vision holds and stays with me.

Behind the buildings on the main street runs the Price River, criss-crossed by bridges and walking trails. A young couple strolls along the river path pushing a baby carriage. Two gray-haired women who appear to be in their 80's stand in gingham cotton house dresses having an animated conversation over a white picket fence.

I stop at the post office and mail my package and head back onto Highway 9 through Spanish Fork Canyon.

Coincidentally, just a few weeks after mailing the package at the Post Office, I meet Ron from Helper at an economic development meeting. He shares his vision of the town as a thriving arts community and goose bumps raise on my arms. Before a month has passed, I find myself leading a visioning exercise in this small railroad town where the voices of the community express their desire to become an arts district. The experience of facilitating this discussion of an arts community foreshadows my future work with establishing arts districts in Colorado.

⌒

The next day, Ron drives up to meet me in Salt Lake City. As I approach the Marriott Hotel where he's staying across from the Salt Palace Convention Center, I see him pacing anxiously in the lobby through the glass doors. When he sees me, he begins speaking impulsively and anxiously, "I need to talk to you!" He grips my arm a little too firmly and guides me through the revolving doors outside. I feel uncomfortable as we wait for the traffic light to cross the street. I suggest a few places we might eat but he's so distracted that I decide on a place myself, and we walk a few short blocks to the restaurant.

As soon as we're seated, he begins. "You must stop living out of your Day Planner." He continues, "And you need to have a life outside of work!" This personal familiarity from a casual business acquaintance is uncomfortable and unnerving to me, but I feel I need to listen because he's so alarmingly earnest. I attempt to redirect our conversation back to our work in Helper. I ask how the community vision for the arts district is progressing.

Ron doesn't seem to hear my question and throughout dinner continues talking about living life scheduled around meetings. Repeated attempts at redirecting the conversation back to work is a lost cause. I find I'm ready for it to end. I don't know what to make of his strange behavior and begin to formulate an exit strategy.

As we walk back to the hotel, he repeats again that I shouldn't be living my life out of my Day Planner- that there's more to life than work. "I'll call you in the morning before I head home to Helper," he persists.

Walking back to the parking garage a few blocks away, I feel unsettled and disturbed by the evening's conversation and by the frenetic look and sound of Ron's voice. His behavior frightens me for some reason.

I arrive at the office the following morning, early as usual. That's my deal. When the phone begins to ring I don't pick up, preferring to concentrate on reading mail and writing reports. Life returns to normal as I settle into my routine and busy work life. After several days I begin to feel more grounded in the familiar patterns of planning and meetings and community work.

I put in long days - I glance at the clock, it's 10pm on a Friday night - time to go home. I crawl into bed and when I wake up the next morning, I realize it's time to clean the house. Noticing the daily newspapers are stacked up on the dining room table, unread, I gather them to toss them in the trash, determined to focus on getting my house in order.

However, as I begin to throw the papers in the recycling, something stops me- an instinct, a hunch? For some mysterious reason it feels extremely important to read the papers before tossing them. I've become more accustomed to listening to and trusting this internal voice and my instincts now. It's become second nature to do so. I brew a pot of coffee and sit down with the newspaper stack, skimming the headlines and the obituaries.

When the pile is nearly finished I'm brought to an abrupt halt. I stare in stunned disbelief at one of the obituaries -- Ron's. My stomach heaves and it's hard for me to breathe, my heart is pounding wildly. I read that he was found dead in his room at the Marriott Hotel the morning after we had dinner. With a sinking feeling in my heart, I realize that his final words, the last words of his life, may have been spoken to me. I ignored the ringing of my phone the morning after we had dinner. Was Ron calling? And I wonder once again what compelled him to make a 2-hour drive to meet me and speak to me face to face to deliver what at the time seemed like a bizarre message. Haunting.

Once again I have a clear and forceful feeling that I'm being given another message, a directive. I've given up my watch. Now I'm being told to give up my Day Planner too? Seriously? I feel I have no choice but to do so. The final words in someone's life are likely infused with extra karmic weight. It certainly seems that way to me.

That morning I decide to change the trajectory of my life. I see Ron as a messenger leading me to a choice I need to make. Perhaps he already had one foot through to another dimension and with it, had clear vision.

Who am I and where do I belong? What should I be doing with my life? These questions pursue me.

13

PEYOTE
MEDICINE

*"I believe much trouble and blood would
be saved if we opened our hearts more."*

Chief Joseph (1840–1904)

Driving southeast on Highway 9 just past Wellington, out of the corner of my eye I see what appears to be a Madonna and Child. I look again and see a native american man and woman sitting in the sagebrush on the side of the road. A mirage? It's a blistering hot day. I pull over and offer them water.

They tell me they're on their way to the reservation in the Four Corners area of Utah, Colorado, New Mexico and Arizona, but they've been stranded on the side of the road for hours. I'm on my way to Moab. They ask if they can ride with me. I tell them to hop in.

The woman, named Anna, appears to be about nine months pregnant. They're trying to get to the Navajo reservation for the birth of her baby. After her brother Thomas tells me some of the details of her story, I remember reading about her in the Salt Lake Tribune. The police found her in an alley, beaten, unconscious, and raped, about nine months ago. Her family tracked down her brother Thomas on the rodeo circuit. When he came to her side she was still in a coma. He chanted her back to life, he tells me, and because of that, in his tradition, he became her lifelong protector and guardian.

Anna tells me Thomas is a songwriter for the Navajo nation. He replies that he's just a rodeo cowboy and proudly shows me his silver belt buckle as proof. He shares with me he used "peyote medicine" to invoke me to stop so they could get home. Anna tells me she's annoyed with him for doing so and is vocal about it until she falls asleep in the back seat.

We stop for gas in Green River and give her lots of water to drink. We buy hamburgers and coke for the remainder of the ride. Anna sleeps most of the way.

I can't be sure if Thomas Emerson is his real name or not. He sings native songs out loud on our drive, occasionally singing a line in English, glancing at me sideways and laughs out loud when I notice. I ask to know the meanings of his words but he won't tell me. He just smiles. He's charming. He asks if I'm married and tells me he'd like to be my boyfriend. This makes me laugh out loud. He laughs with me.

Glancing in my rear-view mirror after I drop them off, I see him standing on the side of the road sliding the crisp $20 bill I've given him into the pocket of his levi's. I chuckle to myself as I think about his Peyote medicine, feeling still somewhat under his spell and somehow blessed by his songs.

14

SYNCHRONICITY

"Synchronicity is an ever present reality for those who have eyes to see."

Carl Jung (1875–1961)

My bare feet are tucked beneath me on the couch in my therapist's office while I sit and wait for her to make a cup of hot green tea. Her office holds a desk, bookcase, chair and couch under a curved bay window on the second floor of a historic home on South Temple Street. The immense, old shade tree outside provides a backdrop beyond the open window, with the sound of leaves rustling as a breeze drifts through. I feel as if I'm inside a treehouse here and it makes me feel young again.

Unintended tears roll down my face as I tell Theresa the dream about my father's death. He appeared to me one night from his hospital bed in Fremont, California. It was 1991. He is dying of cancer and has fallen and broken his hip trying to get out of his chair in front of the television.

In my dream, the night after I'm told of his passing, I merge with him in his hospital room. It's amazing. I know his thoughts and feel his emotions as if they are my own. I'm inside his body and in his heart and his mind.

He (we) sit up on the edge of the hospital bed and I think, but this isn't possible! He has a broken hip. In front of us is a doorway filled with a brilliant, radiant white light. We can barely make out the movements and outlines of human figures in the light and our curiosity is aroused. We stand and walk toward the door of light as one. But as my father walks through, I'm not able to. I'm left behind, standing at the edge of the hospital bed. And even though our bodies are now separated, I continue to share his thoughts and see and feel exactly what he's feeling on the other side of the doorway. As he passes over, we recognize his parents, his brothers and sisters, my mother's parents and all those he loved who've passed ahead of him. We're filled with an indescribable joy to see them all again!

When I wake from the dream I lay in bed in wonder. I'm struck with the finality that my beloved father is gone, yet strangely, I don't feel grief or sadness. It's bittersweet because his joy remains with me. Is this what it's like when we leave our bodies, I wonder? What a beautiful experience and how fortunate I am that he shared the passing of his physical life with me!

Finding a journal entry the morning following the dream, I read, "it is the soul's body of light that continues after death." Where did the words from this journal entry come from? Was he speaking to me? Indeed, I saw these souls through my father's eyes. It was wondrous and real.

I'm now flooded with memories of my father. The summer heat lightning storms in Minnesota are hard to describe but if you've lived in the Midwest in the summer, you know exactly what I mean. When I was growing up we moved many times, following my father's career around the country. He worked in the aerospace industry in the missile defense program following World War II. Looking back, it seems we moved every two years. Me and my siblings became very good at making new friends wherever we lived. Our childhood friends had a difficult time pronouncing our last name with its ten letters and three syllables, so they called us the "Rhino" family. Eleven rhinos.

One of my friends, who knew I collected rhinos, gave me a music box as a gift with an adult and baby rhino and it played the tune "You Light Up My Life." It reminds me of me and my father. After my father died, the music box would start to play randomly from the other room. It happened frequently, and for me it served as a signal, a reminder, that he was always with me, no matter where I was living.

⁓

Back on the couch in my therapist's office, I realize our hour is over. Theresa hands me her card with the date and time of our next appointment written on the back. I tuck it in my pocket along with a book she's given me by Jean Shinoda Bolen, "The Tao of Synchronicity." I walk outside to drive to the airport to catch a flight to California.

The flight is uneventful. I read from the book she gave me.

> *"For those who have felt the power of events, dreams, and meetings that seem to contain meanings deeper than themselves, it can be a window on a world larger and more whole than the world of logical reasoning and concrete facts."*

I feel connected to the words written on the pages of this little paperback book, and this great thinker and writer of thoughts. Her words comfort me and validate my experiences.

When the plane touches down in San Diego, I realize I've forgotten to think about ground transportation to the Hotel Del Coronado where the conference I'm attending is being held. I close my eyes and an image flashes in my mind's eye of a short elderly man in a red jacket wearing a black hat with a silver whistle on a cord around his neck.

My power of visualization has always been fairly strong, but it's super-charged now since my return from Germany. So seeing a clear image of the man in the red jacket when I meditate doesn't surprise me.

I gather up my suitcase from baggage claim and walk outside. There, standing at the curb, is the man in the red jacket and black hat. Chuckling, I give him the address of my destination. He blows his whistle and motions for me to wait under an awning, informing me that a van will be by to get me shortly. He turns to help the next traveler.

A large white passenger van arrives and a young man greets me and loads my suitcase in the back, chatting rapidly all the while. I look inside and see I'm his only passenger. This guy is extremely talkative, about nothing in particular, and I'm feeling a bit annoyed that my silent space is being interrupted. I want to hold onto silence more and more these days, and the intrusion of meaningless chatter and the noise of the outside world isn't easy for me to digest just now.

Abruptly, a clear voice interrupts my thoughts and instructs me to listen and "be here now." Did Ram Dass just come in? I laugh and tell myself to listen and pay attention.

When the driver learns I've flown in from Utah he tells me about his large Catholic family, elaborating in enthusiastic detail about each sibling, explaining to me that he's the youngest child. I hear about his college classes and his goals after school and my mind begins to wander away again.

The voice in my head returns again, challenging me to "be here now!" I re-engage, listening to the driver as he provides detailed descriptions of some of his siblings. I can relate to this a bit. I have eight siblings myself. Redirecting my attention to him once again I hear him talking about his visits to Utah every year to see his oldest sister who "practices some kind of unusual type of transpersonal psychology."

His last statement grabs my attention just as if a bucket of ice water has been poured on my head. I'm suddenly chilled. I ask his sister's name and he replies, "Theresa Holleran."

I burst out laughing and stare out the window in wonder and disbelief. Theresa's brother is watching me curiously in the rear-view mirror. I catch his eye and suggest he pull the van over to the side of the road.

"I was with your sister this morning," I tell him. Now suddenly this talkative guy is at a loss for words. His mouth is actually hanging open! I reach into my pocket and hand him her business card with her hand written note on the back, with the date and time of our next appointment. He's stunned. So am I. I wish I'd captured a photo of his face at that moment. Grinning, I put my head in my hands. Before pulling back onto the road he takes out his cell phone, calls his sister and leaves a message for her telling her what's just transpired.

What was the last thing she said to me as I walked out the door earlier today? Oh yes, it was, "I'm going home now to write about synchronicity." Ha!

15

CREATIVITY

"Creativity is intelligence having fun."

Albert Einstein (1879–1955)

As children, we dream and imagine how our life will be when we grow up. For me, I imagined becoming a nun and eventually a saint assisting others with their worldly concerns, surrounded by golden light and wearing a halo. Undoubtedly, this was my vision because my heroines were nuns and saints as a child raised by a Catholic family and attending parochial schools. I collected beautifully illustrated Holy Cards. They were my prized possessions! I loved their artistic imagery. Studying the illustrations depicted in those cards through paintings from the Renaissance period show women with rapturous blissful faces, reflecting love and enlightenment. The saints' lives inspired me with their good works as unselfish servant leaders.

My mother reinforced these dreams and every night at bedtime she'd remind me to get on my knees and say my prayers.

Learning about the lives of saints and their mythic stories caused me to think about the qualities of prayerfulness, solitude and noble deeds in my earliest years, and fostered my admiration of sacrifice and devotion to a cause. These noble ideals became embedded in my psyche.

As a child, I also began to cultivate my identity as an artist. When I started the first grade, I discovered a full box of unbroken crayons inside my desk on the first day of school. Every day I raised my hand and asked Sister Mary Jane when we were going to draw. Creativity seemed an integral part of my human nature.

I could visualize and imagine a world designed exactly as I wanted it to be. My world was a fascinating, enthralling, exciting and a magical place to be, filled with never ending happiness and love. I believed in the power of visualization. It was genuine and real.

Of course the end of innocence comes as it always does. I never imagined I'd be propelled into the darkened waters of struggle to face as a young woman and as a single mother. Or that I'd be forced to return to work when my baby was ten days old to pay for diapers, formula and baby food, rent and child care. Those were the days when women weren't allowed to use sick leave after giving birth, because you weren't "sick," we could only use vacation leave. I had ten days of it. I thank God for my sweet friend, Deborah Nourse, for watching my ten-day-old baby for me when I returned to full-time work. I cried every morning when I dropped her off and I held her in my arms all night long.

I never imagined I'd eat Gerber baby food strained peas for dinner because my daughter didn't like them and it was the only food left in my apartment. I could never have imagined I'd be fired from a menial clerical job because I was an "unwed" mother. Nor could I ever have imagined the pain, scorn, and burden of responsibility I felt because I'd bravely made the decision to keep my baby and endure the judgment of others, even after I married her father. The gift in this I know now was the development of an ability to let go of the need for approval from others.

What was real for me was the joy of bringing a beautiful life into the world. What was real for me was the unconditional love of this child and the joy of motherhood.

I never imagined any love could be greater than the love I felt for my father until I became a mother and knew a mother's love. I discovered a deeper sense of love that would continue to grow greater throughout her life, defying boundaries or definition. I learned that love wasn't always kind, and that it could break my heart. I learned a broken heart is resilient and can grow larger and stronger. And through the eyes of my child, I came to see and remember my own child-like nature, one of wonder and trust and hope for the future.

It's a painful journey on the way to maturity. It comes from exploring the oceanic depths through the work of the soul. I not only survived this arduous rite of passage; I've grown strong and have thrived. My first baptism was of water. My second was by fire.

—

Time has flown by. My wondrous baby girl has blossomed and grown into womanhood, graduated from college and law school and married a wonderful man.

I'm taking a painting class in Boulder Colorado with my favorite art and meditation instructor. We begin each class with 15 minutes of silent meditation -- meditation on a blank canvas. My instructor, Joan, taps me on the shoulder to tell me to step back and look at what I've painted, telling me she thinks it's complete. It's a painting of myself standing on a mountain holding a baby in my arms as I'm about to step over a dangerous chasm. My late husband is leaning from a cloud, with his hand touching my shoulder. She adds, "I think you're channeling again."

My grandchild appeared to me before he was ever conceived.

I see that I'm connecting to something beyond myself and that something out there in the field of possibility was knocking on my door, asking me to open up and welcome it in again. I first experienced this with my friend David and the series of events that led me on the spiritual pilgrimage with Marianne.

As I stood before my easel, I remember the line from a poem by Jalaluddin Mevlana Rumi, a 13th Century Persian poet, Islamic dervish and Sufi mystic, that goes something like this:

"Come out of the circle of time, into the circle of love."

When I am in my process of creation, I lose track of time and connect with an essence of love and a divine creative spark ignites. My access point in this creative space begins with meditation on a blank canvas.

There is something about being engaged in creative pursuits that makes time stand still for me like it did at 3:15. Einstein is known to have said that time is relative and flexible and that the dividing line between past, present and future is an illusion.

A few months after completing the painting of me holding my grandchild, my daughter informed me she was pregnant. And so it is. I am grateful to have learned how to leave the circle of time and enter the circle of love.

Standing with arms wide open, I declare, "bring it!"

16

ALCHEMY

"Alchemy is really the secret tradition of the redemption of spirit from matter."

Terrence McKenna (1946–2000)

My home in the mountains near Park City overlooks a valley with scrub oak, a meandering mountain stream, and a golf course. It sits in a mountain meadow, a bowl, surrounded by mountain peaks. I bought this place because of a large round window I'd seen several times while meditating and asking for guidance. At the time, I was looking for a new home away from the noise of the city.

It is the same window and the same shafts of sunlight that appear in my dreams in Germany, and appears again in a guided meditation with Theresa. I know I belong here, at least for now.

This mountain valley surrounding my home is alive with birds, deer, foxes and a moose cow and calf I can see along the creek below at dusk. A tapping sound outside my window garners my attention where a woodpecker is drilling into the exterior wood looking for food.

Barbara Joy, my youngest sister, is with me, taking a break from her family and some personal challenges facing her at home. She's the mother of two with another baby on the way. We've always been close. When she was born, my mother let me pick her name.

She asks if I will read her Tarot cards. I know she's struggling with some decisions she needs to make. I've been playing with these cards for a while now, loving their imagery, their symbolism and their history. I agree, hoping it will help her somehow. Before we begin I close my eyes and enter a state of meditation so I can clear my thoughts. I say a prayer and ask for a higher power to give me "guidance" to respond to her questions and give her the loving support she needs now. I explain to her that when I begin a reading, I acknowledge the elements of nature and the four directions to ground myself. She asks what that means and I explain.

The medicine wheel comes from indigenous people who live close to the land, I tell her. We've been told that one of our paternal ancestors is from a tribe in the Great Lakes region of North America. The four elements are earth, wind, water and fire.

Just as I say the word "fire," a bolt of lightning explodes directly above the skylight, lighting up the room through the large windows surrounding us. An explosive crack of thunder makes the house shudder. Barbara's eyes register surprise. "Are you a witch?" she asks. We burst out laughing. "Our brothers have always said so!" I retort.

Just as we all know we have the ability to develop our own greater personal awareness, so too are we contained within a larger field of awareness. While this larger field is invisible, like the atmosphere and the air we breathe, it's just as real. Sometimes these fields appear in dream states, in contemplative practices, in the stories we tell, in our myths and our waking life.

I've learned now that these fields of awareness have neither an inside nor an outside. Like our atmosphere, they permeate everything like electromagnetic waves or vibrations. They exist regardless of time, space or physical separation. This is illustrated when we hear from or feel the presence of people long distances away or those who've passed beyond this mortal life, just as my father appeared to me after he transitioned from this physical life to the next. Just as we consist of ideas, feelings, thoughts and soul, as much as we are made of matter and substance or blood and bones, so too exist these invisible fields that we are part of.

We have the ability and opportunity to follow outer world events and examine our own inner feelings. Instead of simply responding or reacting to events taking place in our physical world, we can develop a practice to notice them and to ask what they might mean in our pathway of personal growth and development. We can view them as information, questions or signs.

I've been playing with this concept. For me, every feeling, thought, movement and experience can be simultaneously an inner and an outer event. So it should be no surprise to me that when I invoked the word "fire" in the card reading with my sister, the field of possibility responded. Either that, or it was another bizarre meaningful coincidence.

This is one of the reasons why all great traditions and teachers instruct us that mindfulness practice and meditation are important to our development, the growth of our souls and for the greater good. When we're doing our inner work, we're also working with the world's energy fields and the collective consciousness. And just as world events affect us personally, our personal work affects the world. I constantly remind myself to meditate so that my impact on the world will be positive.

After Barbara turns in for the night, I shuffle the deck and pull one card to meditate on its archetypal image before I go to bed. It's the Empress Card. The phrase "Self-Transcendence" immediately pops into my head. What does that mean?

I reach for my journal and pen. I write, "the capacity to expand personal boundaries."

I continue to write, "the entire spectrum of human experience, including connection with the mystical and unexplainable experiences that go beyond our small mind's ability to comprehend and understand." Live in mystery, I remind myself.

17

DISCOVERY

"Synchronicity is the Universe saying YES!"

Unknown

The telephone on the kitchen wall rings, startling me, interrupting my evening meditation. I wonder if I should just let it ring. Then I chastise myself that this could be God calling and so I answer.

On the other end of the line I recognize my friend Emily's voice. I met Emily on the spiritual pilgrimage to England and Ireland with Marianne. We have shared common experiences and practices.

She tells me there's been a report of a rapist in her neighborhood and she's seen a man matching the description looking in her basement apartment window. She asks if she can spend the night with me because she's afraid to be alone.

After I hang up the phone, I wonder if I have the capacity to give the love and attention she deserves and needs tonight. Twelve months have passed since I walked away from my corporate job and took a leap of faith. I was given many amazing opportunities to develop new programs, to develop my leadership skills and make a contribution to hundreds of communities across several states. I came to realize I was longing for something more, something more fulfilling for my soul. I've embraced radical trust, standing with open arms to receive the invitation for the next chapter of my life. My house has been on the market for over a year without a single offer. I just mailed in the last payment and my bank account is depleted. I haven't been in a financial situation as scary or risky as this since my daughter was a baby. Yet strangely, I'm trusting the process and I'm not afraid.

I tell myself, if this were my daughter calling for help I'd want someone to be there for her, to offer her a safe space, to sit with her. I have never been able to win a battle against my maternal instincts.

While I wait for Emily to make the drive up Parleys canyon,

I return to my meditation. A voice comes through after a few minutes of silence, crisp and clear, "Tell Emily to go back to school." I'm becoming better at listening now and getting accustomed to the mysterious voice that speaks to me.

Emily tells me that she hasn't been feeling her usual "take on the world" self since the freak tornado in Salt Lake City earlier in the year. That's when it began, she explains, the feeling of being off-balance and questioning why she's here and wondering about her purpose in life.

She takes it well when I deliver the message I've received that she could go back to school. Emily tells me I'm the third person to tell her that this week! She opens up about what she thinks she should study and why. We delve more deeply into what she's truly passionate about and she describes her love for creative writing and tells me about the school with the writing program that most intrigues her. It's in Boulder, Colorado, at a place called Naropa.

More than listening, I'm watching her animated face and listening to the quality of her voice as she talks about Allen Ginsburg and Jack Kerouak and some gibberish about a school for disembodied poets. I sense this is a good path for her to pursue. As I listen and cross into the kitchen to fix us something to eat, I notice a stack of mail on the counter.

I haven't opened my mail for weeks because I'm relatively certain that they're only bills, which will surely amplify the financial uneasiness going on inside me right now. However something catches my attention- a flyer on top of the pile has the words "Naropa" across the front. I pick it up and show it to Emily. How strange, I think, I've never heard of Naropa until tonight and here's a flyer in the mail addressed to me.

"This weekend is a weekend of free classes!" she squeals

with her characteristic positive enthusiasm. "Let's go!" she says and I laugh at her- explaining I can't afford the gas or the overnight costs. Not one ever to be deterred, and understanding the magic of the moment, Em exclaims, "I'll buy the gas and pay for our lodging if you drive..."

—

Boulder is 496 miles east of Park City. The first 60 miles of the journey are over the mountains to Evanston Wyoming as I-80 winds through hills. Oak brush, outcrops of rock and clusters of aspen dot the landscape. It's fall, a stunning time of year in the mountains, and the hills are bathed in brilliant crimson and gold. After that, heading east, it's hundreds of miles of wheatgrass, sage and tumbleweeds and an occasional small herd of antelope- and lots of wind!

When we reach Laramie it feels like we're almost there; only an hour and a half left to drive if we take the "short cut" over Highway 287 along the back roads through Loveland and Longmont. We have miles of time to talk about both important and menial life stuff. We remember the last time we traveled together and fondly reflect on meditating in Stonehenge and Glastonbury Tor with the sage John Michele and our mighty companion, Marianne. Apparently this has bonded us together as pilgrims for life. Here we are once again acting like spiritual pilgrims on a quest, this time in the Rocky Mountains on the road to Boulder.

—

When I decided to request a severance package after 23 years with the power company, I took a leap of faith that this voice that had been guiding me would continue to guide me into the next chapter of my life. It never occurred to me that the voice that had been so extraordinarily powerful and clear, would then go silent for a year.

In that agonizingly long space of silence in my life, I was drawn into a deeper meditation practice and profound surrender to the concept of radical trust. I vowed to myself not to make a decision about any next steps in my life until I heard a very clear YES. I've discovered that in listening to the messages of synchronicity, dreams and meaningful coincidences, my life is richer and more fulfilling and I feel much more present and fully alive. I can't and I won't go back to a life or soul unfulfilled.

On my refrigerator, and on the mirror in my bathroom, I post a saying my friend Pam has written down for me during a time of hard questioning about my life and future. This saying becomes a prayer and lifeline.

> *"When you walk to the edge of all the light you have and take that first step into the darkness of the unknown, you must believe that one of two things will happen. There will be something solid for you to stand upon, or you will be taught how to fly." -Patrick Overton*

～

Emily and I arrive in Boulder after dark has fallen and drive around looking for a motel with a vacancy sign. We find one on Canyon Road and check ourselves in. The next morning we find our way to Naropa and take one of the free art classes working with found objects and assemblage. Afterwards we give ourselves a self-guided tour of the Naropa campus on Arapahoe Street and sit in the Maitri meditation rooms.

I'm beginning to feel as if I've arrived at a place that's been waiting for me. It isn't long, perhaps an hour into meditation, that I realize this place is for my soul's journey and it took Emily's crisis to enable me to find my way here.

When we return to Utah, I complete the application forms, submit reference letters and am notified that my credits from the University of Utah are accepted. After the prescribed requisite hour phone interview, it is decided; I am accepted for winter semester. I place the receiver in the cradle of the phone when the interview is over, but before I can let go, the phone rings and I pick it up again. My friend and real estate agent, Judy's happy voice greets me. She reports with delight that we've received a full price offer on my home from a pre-qualified buyer. It has taken a year, but the clear affirmative "YES" I've been waiting for has finally arrived!

When we acknowledge our own powerlessness to control things, and we humble ourselves to ask for help and divine intervention, the guidance appears. Doorways open before us, inviting and welcoming us to walk through.

18

LETTING GO

"When I let go of what I am, I become what I might be. When I let go of what I have, I receive what I need."

Tao Te Ching – Lao Tzu (601 BC)

Seriously! How much stuff can one person accumulate in a couple of years? This is the third time I've practiced giving everything away and starting over. My dishes, stemware and small kitchen appliances are going to my friend Suzanne's retreat center, The Edge, in Duchesne. Most of the furniture will be trucked to consignment stores and everything else, including my business suits, to Goodwill.

I have no idea what a 40-something year old woman wears on a campus in Boulder, Colorado. The life of a student? It's been a long time. I decide to keep jeans and tee-shirts, sweaters, coats and boots.

Letting go, I discover, isn't just about the stuff I've accumulated, it's also about aspects of my identity. This includes friends from grade school, colleagues from work, and relationships built through 20 years of engagement in communities across seven states. No more titles or business cards, at least not for now. I feel relieved.

During the course of my career, my profile has become a very public one, sometimes a little too public for the comfort of an introvert like myself. I prefer a good book to a large gathering and small talk. It's a curious thing for me as to why I've been recruited for so many leadership positions. When I'm asked to serve on boards and committees, and asked to chair non-profit and business organizations, I feel humbled but not comfortable in the public eye. But I push through my self-talk and do it anyway. I've been given honors for volunteer work, been on television, featured in advertisements for my employer, and been written about in magazines and newspaper stories.

Public recognition makes me quite self-conscious and uneasy. It's because I don't feel I can take credit for many of my accomplishments. I feel a greater force is always working through me. It's truly not about me. It's about doing good work as a calling. These days, I go to a grocery store or gas station and run into people who know me or seem to recognize me. And as a classic introvert, it's something I have never been comfortable with. In fact, one day as I was trying on bras in Nordstrom, the sales clerk turned and asked, "Aren't you Margaret Hunt? I saw you on TV last night." Wow. That really felt intrusive and uncomfortable.

I'm relieved to know the best thing about moving to Boulder is the opportunity to go unnoticed and fly under the radar, to rediscover and connect with who I truly am and discover what I want to become in this fresh chapter of my life. In this place, I can go to the grocery store in sweats without make-up and my hair in a pony tail and no one will recognize me. Anonymity is freedom, I realize, and there is great power in that. So I drop my list of accomplishments from the past and enter into full-on, curious, real-time-learning student of life mode, preparing for how I might rediscover myself.

The first thing I notice in Boulder is that students at Naropa change their names to Willow and Breeze and Dharma and other interesting monikers. I choose Maggie, in large part because my mother wouldn't let anyone call me anything other than Margaret as a child, so it feels like a small act of disobedience and defiance. It also feels light and playful, more in line with how I feel these days.

I give some thought to starting a sorority here and naming it something like Karma Dharma Ding Dong. The class list reads like a feast from the gods for me. Beginning and Advanced Meditation Practice, History of Contemplative Practices, Creative Writing, Thangka Painting, Transpersonal Psychology, Art as Healing.

I haven't been in Boulder long before discovering they do some pretty weird stuff here, like bury placentas under the trees in the courtyard on campus and relocate prairie dogs to protect the green space around the city. The city hires farmers to bring their goats to eat the grass along roads coming into town because it's better for the environment. But this weird is refreshing and seems liberating after living for so long in Utah, with its conservative mindset and traditional thinking. Two bookends: Salt Lake City and Boulder, methinks. Two ends of a spectrum of being in the world. Both with a history of spiritual movements; one Mormon, the other Buddhist. There is value in the richness of this spectrum of beliefs.

Naropa's campus and curriculum are deliberately infused with world teachers and spiritual practice. I meet a former Catholic priest in my ethics class and sit in meditation with Jewish and Buddhist practitioners. A journal entry from that period includes a note from a lecture and a story in which Buddha is asked to reassure his followers about the existence of God. His reply is that the only viable answer requires a personal journey, a truth which resonates with me. I'm reassured that it's ok to continue on this journey of personal and spiritual discovery in my life.

I often hear Boulder being described as a place where hippies flocked and a place of liberal thinking. But that fails to recognize the influence of Eastern ideology on Boulder's culture. When he was exiled from Tibet to India, the 14th Dalai Lama called upon Chogyam Trungpa Rinpoche, a Tibetan Buddhist Monk, to help spread his teachings.

After studying English, Rinpoche eventually received a scholarship to study comparative religion at Oxford. He returned to the U.S. in 1970 and founded what is now Shambhala International, an institution teaching the noblest Buddhism principles to Westerners. He also taught at Colorado

University in Boulder in the 1970's and later founded Naropa Institute, the first accredited Buddhist Institution in the U.S.

Rinpoche coined the term "crazy wisdom" to describe the knowledge one gains from finding no answers. One significant thing about Shambhala teachings is the notion or acknowledgement that answers are elusive. This rings true for me. Rather than answers, I'm more comfortable with a direction, like the suggestion to become an explorer, to look inward or to follow a meaningful coincidence.

19

VOICE

"There is a voice that doesn't use words. Listen."

Rumi (1207-1273)

It happens when I'm asleep. It happens when I'm awake. A firm, loud voice shouts "Margaret!" and wakes me from a deep sleep tonight. I sit straight up in bed, look around, my heart is pounding, and as always happens, I'm absolutely certain someone else is in the room. Yet there's no physical presence there. The past leaves scars and I wonder if this could be one from my troubled married life. At the same time, I also trust and feel that something deeper is at work here.

"Don't be afraid! You can make no mistakes!" the voice shouts another time. This message surprises me since I was raised with the concepts of venial and mortal sins that required confession and the need to be forgiven by a priest who assigned penance as atonement for my sins. This concept of "you can make no mistakes" is intriguing to me.

After a prolonged period of hearing this voice again and again, self-doubt begins to gnaw at me. I ask myself if it's possible I'm losing my mind. Hearing voices has been described as a psychological disorder in some of my readings about spirituality and collective consciousness.

I call my daughter Nicole who's in law school on the east coast, forgetting it's two hours later there. Her sleepy voice answers and then I realize it's midnight in Maryland. "Oh, I'm sorry, I woke you," I apologize. "It's ok, mom," she replies, being supportive. I describe the most recent occurrences and ask her if she thinks it's possible I'm losing my mind. "I don't know" she replies, "Have you talked to Theresa?" I ramble on and she listens, remaining patient and I thank her and apologize again. "I love you mom," she says sweetly.

Another thing is happening frequently while I sleep. The phone rings one time. The ring tone is the sound of a bell. I awaken and wait for the second ring. It doesn't ring again. It's always just one ring and it seems so lucid and real. This has been going on for months and I wonder if it's a message or messenger. But whatever it is, I'm not getting it. Tonight when I turn in for bed, I'm going to meditate and ask the caller to reveal her or himself to me this time. But the trick doesn't work. I decide I will remain open minded and live in the mystery.

It takes me 30 minutes on my bike to get to school from my home in Gunbarrel, an unincorporated area of Boulder County. I'm 20 pounds lighter now and feel engaged in life again. Each class begins and ends with meditation. My painting style has completely changed. Meditation on a blank canvas is my entry point and I wait until colors or symbols present themselves before I begin. I trust that my hands and mind are being used as a vehicle for expression of something larger than what my small mind can conjure up. Occasionally, Joan, the instructor, will tap me on the shoulder gently and tell me to step back and look at what I've done. "You're channeling again," she says. It surprises me the first time she says that to me. I accept it now, recognizing that she may know something about me that I'm not aware of myself.

After the Spiritual Warrior class in Shambhala Hall, I check my backpack to make sure I have my sketchbook and journal before I walk out into the sunshine, past the bookstore across the parking lot. I cut behind the student housing on the University of Colorado campus and briskly walk the short distance to the Boulder bike path and river. My favorite granite boulder is unoccupied and I begin sitting meditation with the sound of the river, letting go of my thoughts, focusing only on breath.

"Notice me," the juniper seems to say, standing on one leg with outstretched limbs. "Notice me," the cascading water replies. Sitting, struck silent in their living presence, I observe nature's way of simply being in the world, seen or unseen, always unaffected and unpretentious. Saturated in color, moving folds of maroon and saffron robes appear behind the leaves and tree trunks as Tibetan monks walk by, heads lowered, voices either whispered or diffused by the sound of the water. This peaceful place is one of my favorite in the world, where the hum of the water seems to intuitively quiet my thoughts.

Alert now, I think of something my writing teacher Leland said when I wrote about the unusual experiences I've been having. "You live in different realms of reality, Miss Maggie. You have amazing stories and you must write." I feel truly heard and acknowledged and safe here on this campus with these teachers. I also love having the freedom of stretches of unstructured time. Awareness and observation permeate my life now.

I highly recommend taking long breaks from watches, technology and electronic devices, television and business suits of armor. This opportunity to go deeply into spiritual study and meditation practice is a gift we can give ourselves. I recall Marianne saying something like, "Sacred silence writes the miracle."

When we practice silencing our internal chatter and manage the outside noise, guidance shows up for us. This voice we learn to recognize as our very own is coming from our Higher Self, which is in communion with the Divine. It's our task to let go, to follow this voice and hear its demands, guidance, and wise counsel.

20
SURRENDER

"There are as many pillows of illusion as flakes in a snow storm. We wake from one dream into another dream."

Ralph Waldo Emerson (1803–1882)

Pam phones to tell me her husband Glen has advanced lung cancer. He doesn't have much time left. Oh my, my dearest of friends. There's nothing I can do but meditate and pray. This is the letting go stuff that none of us want to do. I call him and ask if I can keep in touch with him when he's on the other side. "I don't know," he replies with his characteristic honesty. He adds, "Put blue marbles under your bed." Pam attributes this comment to the pain meds he's taking, but I don't care. I put blue marbles under my bed anyway.

My girlfriend Pat Martin calls the next day to tell me she's been diagnosed with mesothelioma. She thinks she probably inhaled asbestos at one of the power plants while she was the human resource manager at the Power Company. The longest anyone's lived with this is five years if they're healthy and not a smoker. Shit. Shit. Shit. I don't want to accept that we'll be separated from the physical presence of those we love. Not now. Not this young. This letting go is too personal, too painful.

There's a kind and gentle surrender to be found from listening to the words and voice of David Whyte when he recites his poem, *The Well of Grief*. I copy his poem and put it on my refrigerator to remind me not to forget the power of its message.

> *"Those who will not slip beneath the still surface on the well of grief, turning down through its black water to the place we cannot breathe, will never know the source from which we drink, the secret water, cold and clear, nor find in the darkness glimmering, the small round coins thrown by those who wished for something else."*

Some forms of meditation practice tell us to focus on the breath to control the distractions of the mind and our incessant habit of "thinking." This has become my preferred practice. My two friends have been struck in the lungs. They can no longer take breath for granted. Not only do I recommit to my meditation practice, but I'm grateful for the simple ability to breathe today as I think about impermanence and change.

I consciously attempt to get away from the constant incessant chatter of my thoughts, away from everything I've been taught by teachers or read in books. In silent meditation, I find peace and harmony, safety and stillness. We hear what we're meant to hear. We take it in, we internalize what's right for us in that particular moment. I'll not take a breath for granted now.

When I was young in my awkward pre-teens, I dreaded walking up to the altar at the front at Church to receive Holy Communion because I could feel people looking at me. It was painful and crippling to be shy and skinny. When I was in high school, an awkward and difficult time for most people, I overheard one of my classmates comment, "My God, she's skinny!" That didn't help my self-confidence or self-esteem. It came from someone I admired and liked. I thought we were friends and for that reason it truly hurt me.

I see that same classmate occasionally, and she once began a conversation with a negative comment about someone's appearance. It immediately brought back the painful high school memory. It still hurts. Even when the wounds are healed, the scar of painful memories remains with us. But I didn't say anything to her. Why? Where was my voice? I know she's a good person and I know if I'd approached the subject with her in the right way, I could have been of greater service to her own awareness and personal growth. It's something I continue to work on- to speak up and become better at speaking truthfully in a kind and compassionate way. We are all a work in progress, after all.

There are people we admire or in positions of power who occasionally say cruel things. We're all guilty of that and I remind myself I need to speak up when this happens. I believe the "Me Too" movement is helping. There's power in a chorus of voices. Just look at the 2017 Women's March! It was astonishing to be in the crowd in Denver's Civic Center Park that day with my daughter and family, connecting with minds linked against abuse to women, and to see how this movement spread across the world that day.

One of my supervisors told me early in my career that I needed to speak up – to find my voice. He recommended I enroll in the company's Toastmasters Club. I hated that I was being told I needed to join a club! I'm not a joiner. At the time, I was terrified to speak in front of people. As I discovered, this turned out to be an incredibly supportive group of people which was not at all what I expected. I got comfortable and I learned to trust them. With lots of regular and consistent practice, I became good at speaking and I actually learned to enjoy it. Discovering my "out loud" voice changed me. I discovered I could be funny and speak with purpose and people were interested in me and what I had to say.

In one of the boxes I unpacked after my last move, among the journals and sketchbooks, I found my <u>Best Speaker</u> trophy from my PAL Toastmasters Club from 1983. I cherish that rinky-dink trophy because of what I had to overcome to earn it from my peers, and the skills I developed there have helped me become who I am today.

This notion of voice is interesting to me. There's our literal voice, which we're in control of, and one that I'm now comfortable with. And there's also this other voice – the one that speaks through me and you – the voice of our soul that speaks to us in union with a higher power. And I'm getting more comfortable with that one now too. From A Course in Miracles:

> *"The two voices speak for different interpretations of the same thing simultaneously; or almost simultaneously, for the ego always speaks first. And it speaks the loudest!"*

To hear this profound voice of the Soul or Higher Self, it requires us to quiet the voices in our head from our ego and the distractions and noises so that we can hear that powerful voice within. It wants to be heard. It needs to be heard for our soul's purpose. We need to practice quieting our minds so that we can hear it speak. I believe it's our true voice.

By listening in this way, by silencing our ego, we find inner clarity and purpose. We sleep better. Our mental health improves. We're less stressed. While all these things are valuable benefits, the greatest benefit is our internal alignment for the advancement of our soul's journey.

21

ILLUSIONS

*"If the doors of perception were cleansed
every thing would appear to man
as it is, Infinite. For man has closed
himself up, till he sees all things through
narrow chinks of his cavern."*

William Blake (1757-1827)

My flight to Mexico City is a smooth and uneventful one. The Utah Governor's office has sent me to follow up on his recent visit to explore the possibility of a cultural exchange with Mexico. The taxi ride to the hotel passes through a roundabout, La Reforma, with a massive sculpture and fountain. Surrounding the sculpture today are hundreds of beautiful naked brown women, singing and dancing. I'm not able to get my camera out quickly enough to capture the image, so I save it in my mind. How marvelous it is that these women have the courage to do this in such a public place. This image of naked women dancing and singing in a public town square is a reminder to me that the world is much larger than a city or state or country.

After checking into the hotel, I click on the remote control in my room with fifteen minutes of free time before dinner. It's a riveting scene with Anthony Hopkins and Cuba Gooding, Jr. from the film *Instinct*.

Hopkins, a maximum security prisoner, is holding his psychiatrist (played by Gooding) by the neck shouting, "Who's in control? Are you? Am I? Who's in control? You've never had control! That's an illusion. You think you're free? What has you tied up in little knots? Ambition?"

The scene continues with Hopkins giving Gooding a chance to live if he answers his question correctly. "What have you lost? Write it!" On the third try, Gooding's character gets the answer right. "My illusions" he replies correctly. I'm reminded of Einstein's thought that the dividing line between past, present, and future is an illusion.

Returning to my room after midnight, I'm still wide awake, so I click on the remote again. It's the exact same scene from the movie. Astonishing.

Later, when I'm back at home, I turn on the TV and scroll through the movie menu and see the listing for *Instinct*. Maybe this time I can watch the entire film, I think. I click the menu button for the film. Once again, it's the same exact scene, for the third consecutive time. Ok then! Message received!

Control is an illusion. Time is an illusion. We're part of a bigger deal. Life has become a chorus of meaningful moments and experiences. Seeing the scene again for the third time brings me to tears. It's hard to say what the source of my tears is, other than a realization that there is a power greater than mine, tirelessly and insistently trying to get my attention. I feel a sense of joy and gratitude for this invisible force. I'm able to let down an assumed mantle of leadership and my own illusion that I need to be "in charge" because of some appointed position or job. Again I find myself asking, do I let go of my need to take charge and trust the ability to rely on a force that is greater than my own?

It's amazing and also freeing to feel a connection to this force in the Universe. Observing, participating, transmitting, receiving, absorbing, reflecting, fully in, heart wide open, in surrender. I'm living in a world of life interrupted, change of plans, a larger plan, one requiring surrender, unexpected challenges and sudden inspirations. It takes courage and faith to hold this space in this unpredictable stream of daily life and distraction. Now that I've discovered this space, I'm certain there's no turning back.

———

It's been said that Buddha wants to extract the seed of illusion from our thoughts. What illusions am I holding? I realize that not only should I look at whatever illusions I may believe in, I should also look at my defenses. As humans, we put up buffers or blinders like front and rear bumpers on a car. We put them there to protect ourselves on the bumpy road of life.

These defenses prevent us from being fully alive and vulnerable; from seeing present moment realities and the entire picture of what's present in our lives, or what might be. Please reveal to me my illusions and help me remove my blinders, I pray.

My prayer is interrupted by the faint sound of music, and I follow the sound. It's my music box with the two rhinos and it's playing "You Light Up My Life" again. I think of my father. I think he's letting me know he's here to help me. I wonder if I will ever get used to these spontaneous unpredictable messages from this unseen, unknowable force.

22

FIELDS

"Out beyond ideas of wrong-doing and right-doing, there is a field. I'll meet you there."

Rumi (1207–1273)

Can you imagine the possibility of fields of consciousness crossing time and space, without boundaries? I find myself working on something and discover that someone close to me is working on the same thing. Or that someone I'm thinking about picks up their phone and calls me at the moment I'm thinking of them.

It happened last week when I thought to call my credit union to inquire about my credit card account. My cell phone rings as soon as I have this thought and the credit union employee informs me she's calling about my credit card account. Random?

In another instance, I feel compelled to see the film Interstellar. I don't know why. I don't even know what the movie is about. I'm simply listening and answering the call. Checking my cable TV service, I'm unable to find it on demand. But the message is crystal clear to me and I feel compelled to see this movie for some reason.

Since I can't find it on cable, I hop on the internet and find the DVD in stock at Target. There's a horrific hail storm happening outside. It's late spring and hailstorms are a common occurrence this time of year in the Rockies. But regardless, I get in my car and drive through the hail storm to buy the DVD. Returning home, I discover my DVD player is still in an unpacked storage box in the garage. After locating the right box and unpacking it, I attempt to install the DVD player only to realize I'm missing the right kind of cable to connect it to my TV. Once again I get back in the car and back out in the storm to buy the right type of cable.

Home again, I discover the new cable fits my DVD but it doesn't fit my newer-version flat screen TV. Still determined and undeterred, I get back in the car and drive through the storm to Best Buy to purchase a new DVD player that's compatible with my TV. Is this determination or insanity? Yet

I am so certain of this guiding intuition that I follow it and make three successive trips in a wicked storm. Three!

After watching the movie, I begin to understand why I was guided to do so. The film gives me more information and another perspective about theories of time, about time folding back on itself, and the possibility of going back in time. Einstein speaking?

The next morning I get dressed to meet my daughter for breakfast. Since she loves science fiction, I tell her she needs to see this movie. Laughing, she tells me she watched the movie the night before. It isn't unusual for family members or close friends to share the same thoughts and ideas at the same time. But a credit union employee who I've never met calling me about a credit card when I'm thinking about it? My daughter and I watching the same movie at our respective homes at the same time? I feel as though I should be used to this by now, but these occurrences are still surprising me.

Do our minds meet there, in the field of consciousness that Rumi refers to as a place beyond all right-doing and wrong-doing? Or what's known as one mind, or Big Mind, as Zen Buddhists call it?

—

I typically wake at first light every morning. This morning I follow my inclination to drive to the Rocky Mountain Wildlife Refuge. It takes about five minutes to get there from my home.

When I arrive, the gates are open and deer are grazing in the prairie grasses. My car windows are down so I can hear the sound of birdsong. It's a brisk 45 degrees outside so I turn up the heat to keep my feet warm.

The last time I felt compelled to be here was with my grandchild when we sat on the banks of the ponds, blowing our duck calls. The mallards and geese responded, and swooped in over our heads to our great delight. It was dusk and it wasn't long before we heard coyotes yipping 360 degrees around us. We turned to one another with a look of astonishment mixed with concern and raced back to the car as fast as we could. On another visit we sat within ten feet of a Peregrine Falcon perched on a tree branch beside the road. This connection to nature is one of the surest ways I know to experience the magic and mystery of the great unseen force that guides our physical world. When a wild animal graces us with their unexpected presence, it feels like we're being given a blessing.

Today I absorb the sound of magpie chatter and the song of meadowlark and red-winged black birds. Rounding a bend in the road, I enter the Bison area. On the road ahead is the herd and I approach slowly, cautiously, and with reverence for these magnificent animals. It's springtime and there are bison babies surrounded by protective adults who snort when my car approaches, warning me to keep my distance.

The bison, or American Buffalo, is a symbol of abundance and manifestation in some teachings. I stop with the windows down in the center of a herd to soak in their presence. These enormous animals can weigh up to a ton and a half, with massive heads and humped shoulders, cloaked in capes of shaggy dark fur. I'm reminded that upon our shoulders we either carry burdens or rewards. There are times when I've thought of hard work as a burden rather than a reward.

This morning I offer a prayer of gratitude for my ability to work hard doing work I love, and ask that these efforts be combined with the power of Divine Will. I am entirely ready to be led along the path that is destined for me that I may remain in service to my community. I trust things will happen in the time, manner and means that are best, and that synchronicity serves me both as affirmation and as guideposts.

Mahayana Buddhism teaches followers to stand for the healing of the suffering we see in the world around us. Buddhists have faith that when enlightenment is attained, they are freed from the cycle of reincarnation. When given the choice of whether to choose personal enlightenment and freedom from reincarnation, or service to humanity, His Holiness the Dalai Lama is known to say he will choose reincarnation so that he can be in service to humanity until all are free from suffering. No wonder he's revered and adored!

23

SERVICE

"The best way to find yourself is to lose yourself in the service of others."

Mahatma Gandhi (1869–1948)

At one point in my career, I have been appointed as the Executive Director of the Utah Arts Council, serving in the administration of Governor Jon Huntsman. The National Endowment for the Arts had initiated a new program called Poetry Out Loud. It's a poetry recitation competition for high school students across the United States that encourages kids to memorize and recite poetry. More importantly, it is for them to develop an appreciation for poetry as an art form, both written and spoken word. Each state arts agency is directed to hold a competition, and each state champion will be sent to Washington DC to compete in the national finals, with the winner receiving a $20,000 college scholarship.

Beginning any new program in schools is challenging – working with school bureaucracies and engaging with teachers who've worked hard for years to establish their curriculum. Our public school teachers are largely over-worked and under-paid. Then there's the added difficulty of getting students excited and interested in the art of poetry itself. It can be a herculean effort.

The Endowment is met with some resistance from state arts agencies across the country when they initiate this new program because it's viewed as an underfunded mandate from the federal government. The Endowment counters back that if states don't participate, their federal funding might be in jeopardy. Poetry Out Loud is the passion of the NEA Chairman, a poet himself. Since Endowment funding enables us to reach rural and underserved communities in our state, we decide it's important for us to get on board with this new mandate.

We commit to do the best we can and put our focus on the kids and how we might be able to provide a great learning experience for them in our inaugural year. My colleagues step up to the challenge, as they always do, and reach out to school districts and English teachers and rally support. The Endowment sends representatives to as many states as possible to give encouragement and thank us for taking on this new program.

The final competition is held at Salt Lake City's East High School. I'm visiting with Tony from the NEA in the hallway as the judges are deliberating and selecting the finalists for the last round of competition when a reporter from a daily newspaper approaches me with a question. "What will you do if the winner of this competition is 'undocumented?'" she asks. Her question surprises me and I reply that I don't think it will be an issue because all children are entitled to participate in the public school system and its programs.

This is during the height of an acrimonious national debate over immigration and undocumented people in our country, which is particularly targeted at Mexican immigrants. Some feel the pressures being put on our schools, hospitals and social service agencies has reached a critical crisis point. Others counter that these people are filling jobs in the construction and service industries in restaurants and hotels that otherwise can't be filled, and are necessary contributors to our economy. They assert they are paying social security and taxes into a system that benefits only American citizens and not themselves. And others, including many churches, take a stance for humaneness and care for all people regardless of color, religion, or country of origin.

As I read this journal entry now years later, I realize things haven't changed much in our nation since then. The debate still rages and it's still disheartening.

We learn at the end of the Poetry Out Loud event that the state champion the judges select is indeed undocumented. The following day I re-read the rules for the competition issued by the Endowment. They state that the competition is open to all high school students. We make plans to send our winner to Washington DC to compete in the national finals.

A few days later I receive a phone call from an Endowment attorney who informs me that we cannot send our state winner to the final competition because of her undocumented status. I feel enraged and betrayed.

I pull out the Endowment rules and re-read them again more carefully. They clearly state that every high school student is eligible to participate. So if she can participate, I muse, why can't she represent our state at the national finals? I don't understand. There has to be a solution. I reach out to Senator Orrin Hatch's office. His staff agrees to meet with me and they listen and are understanding. But they posit that the political timing isn't good to fight this particular battle.

I'm not discouraged and I persist. I explore a variety of ways to get our state champion to the finals in Washington, including trains and charter flights. Again I'm told by Endowment attorneys that if we send our state champion to the finals in D.C., by sending her across state borders, I'll be violating federal law. They ask me if I am willing to risk being sent to federal prison for ten years for transporting an undocumented person across state lines. I'm appalled. I don't care about that. I care about her.

We were fortunate to have Tony Chauveaux, a senior manager from the Endowment, as our guest at the state finals. His calm and trusting demeanor and his empathetic voice of reason gave me much reassurance during this struggle.

After much internal anguish, I finally accept and concede defeat on the issue out of concern for her protection and that of her family. I need to break the news to her.

As I sit in her living room with her family, I attempt to

explain why she can't represent our state in the final competition. I share tears and disappointment with her and her parents. She tells me that she's an American. It's all she's ever known - carried across the border as a babe in arms - as a child who recited the Pledge of Allegiance every day in public school.

Feeling helpless, I listen. And then I come to understand from her that her ultimate goal is to win the national competition to get the grand prize - a scholarship - so she can go to college. She'll be the first in her family. Her eye is on the scholarship. A voice inside tells me there is something we can do about this.

I attend the national finals in Washington, D.C. with our first runner-up and her family. Afterwards, in a debriefing meeting with NEA Chairman and representatives from other states, one of my colleagues, Randy Rosenbaum from Rhode Island, asks about the state champion who wasn't allowed to participate in the finals. The Chairman responds that he's not willing to "fall on his sword" over this issue and changes the subject. I remain silent in that moment, somewhat dumbfounded by this response, which seems callous to me. Others in the room speak up on our behalf. While I felt enormously frustrated at the time, I also felt incredible gratitude for my colleagues for speaking up to the Chairman about the perceived unfairness of the situation.

While still holding onto my disappointment, I present the issue to our Governor-appointed advisory board. It's then that I discover there are angels living among us. A council member from the University of Utah appeals to her colleagues on campus and they provide this deserving young woman with a four-year full ride scholarship!

I'm awestruck by this realization that a power much greater than mine is always at work in the Universe. I trust this solution came about not only because of the absolute clarity of this young woman's vision for herself, but also because of the power of the dreams of others who are egalitarian and feel passionately about this challenge to our collective humanity. There are mighty companions among us who want to do the right thing. It's often in difficult times we discover these other heroic hearts who may be sitting quietly beside us until they are summoned into action.

Of all my professional achievements, seeing this young woman graduate from the University with honors is the one that gives me the greatest personal satisfaction. Miracles like this enable us to have confidence in the goodness of others.

While the odds weren't likely this young woman would have won the national competition, her prayers were answered nonetheless. Confronting reality and obstacles with a compassionate heart and trust enabled a calling for a solution I could never have imagined possible.

There are other battles to be fought. While we may not win in the short term, it's important to take a stand for what we know in our hearts to be the honorable course of action. Perhaps the timing isn't right or the powers that be aren't the right beings in power. Nonetheless, we must persist!

24

DIGGING DEEPLY

"Knowing others is intelligence.
Knowing yourself is true wisdom.
Mastering others is strength.
Mastering yourself is true power."

Lao Tzu

Joseph Campbell, arguably the greatest mythologist of our time, was an incredible storyteller. In his writing about the Hero's Journey, he proposes that in an elevated place of thought, we witness our collective power emerging in the world. In this heightened sense of awareness and mindset, we can achieve a balance between our inner and outer world by being in service to others. We become the master of two worlds – both inner and outer. I believe it's time for women to claim our place, our power, our voice, and our creativity and own up to our spiritual mastery. We are today's heroines and mistresses of the future of our planet. We are the complement to the hero's journey.

Campbell asserts that this mastery of two worlds leads to the final state of being - the freedom to live fearlessly, to live in the moment with no concern for the future or regrets of the past. No fear in the moment. No concern for the future. No concern with the past.

Buddha teaches that suffering is inevitable. He also teaches that the same thing that roots our lives in suffering also leads to the way out of suffering, which is self-awareness.

Writing, painting, and meditation are helpful tools in self-awareness. For certain, they are my connection to my most authentic creative self.

And then there's the action of being intentional. I practice setting intentions with my inner and outer work to become the mistress of the two worlds. In truth, we're simply coming home. I tell you, we must all resolve to be more intentional about our soul work and our work in the world.

Besides being more conscious, deliberate, and purposeful, it's crucial that we allow life to unfold with us, magically, moment by moment, and be open to all that it offers, whether expected or not. It is through living in the mystery that we can truly inhabit our authentic selves and harness our greatest power, and the power of the Universe.

From the view of public service with a higher mission of doing work in the world, this intention can simply be summed up as being in service in the moment- whatever that moment looks like.

In my work today I feel fortunate that I'm able to engage with amazing, brilliant and creative people who inspire me, in large and small cities, in mountain towns and frontier communities.

This work is satisfying and fulfilling for me because it's coming from a place of the soul's work; confronting and embracing the good, the bad and the difficult. Let's commit to being more present in honoring and acknowledging the places and means by which we can make a difference.

Looking back, it was challenging to be my most authentic and complete self in the corporate environment, and I found the focus on profits over people had become empty and meaningless work for me. Yet I learned from the experiences I had there, and they helped to refine my choices and the character of who I am and who I'm becoming. These experiences enabled me to take the next steps on my journey, to identify where I needed to learn to say "no" and to be guided by a stronger, more powerful energy. Wisdom is the outcome of our experiences and this wisdom comes from inner growth over time.

In this place along this journey, together, let's practice being in the moment and waiting patiently to listen and pay attention until we hear "YES" before taking action.

I've come to appreciate that every experience I have, whether it's in a dream state, in my mind or in the physical world, or one that drags me into the basement or underworld of my psyche, it's an opportunity for change and growth. But it only works by developing self-awareness to recognize the opportunities being presented.

Let's make the choice to be fully alive and fully present in the present moment. Then miracles will occur naturally as expressions of the Divine.

In one of my journals I come across a notation that remains true for me now. It likely came from the wisdom of the Bhagavad Gita, "The Song of God," a 700-verse Hindu scripture.

> *"Act well without attachment to the fruits of your actions.*
> *Love well without attachment to the fruits of your love."*

Things aren't going well for me today. The sewer has backed up in my basement again. The first time it happened was three years ago. And exactly one year later I went through the angst a second time. Today's backup is the third time in three years. There it is again – the number three – the sign for me to be attentive to the synchronicity of the situation. I know I really have no choice. Yet I'm fed up. I feel like giving up. I hate this shit. Ha!

I confess I'm feeling powerless and small today; the helplessness and despair seem overwhelming. I want to escape under the covers of my bed and break down. I want to give up. I don't have answers. My tank is empty. It's not the big things that get to me, it's these mundane details of life. I need help and I'm neither comfortable nor good at asking for it. When the help is for someone else, it's easy for me to ask. When I need help for myself, that's an entirely different matter.

I wonder if this descent into the sewer is symbolic of a deep cleansing internally inside my house, my house representing the body in which I dwell? I felt those depths had been purged and healed long ago.

I tell myself I should pray and meditate and even those thoughts piss me off. How can I use the energy of my human anger, I ask myself. I decide to call in reinforcements – my powerful fierce allies like the goddess Kali – my daughter, another fierce warrior goddess. She comes right over. Her logical, legal mind is exactly what's needed now. I'm not right in my head.

Where's that voice now when I need it? I ask. It answers immediately. "This is your shit in the basement." I recall Nora from our dream group saying that the basement represents our emotions and deepest darkest places. Has this warrior persona of mine looked in these places lately? I suppose it's time to do so once again.

I step back and let Nicole run the show. She takes charge of the homeowners' representative, the sewer guys, and calls a lawyer friend who specializes in construction defect cases. She's in her element. They discover there's a break in the sewer line six feet under the driveway.

Six feet underground. I'm at a loss for answers and in search of clues for meaning. I rummage through the box of journals and open one of them at random. I read, "I'm at my best when I'm being my creative self." Have I buried my creative self six feet under, I ask myself.

Even after the amount of time I've spent in spiritual exploration, meeting with teachers, spending time at Naropa, and practicing meditation, the cycle of learning begins again. After experiencing transcendent moments, recognizing guidance and learning to trust our inner voice, life appears to be a spiral that puts us back at the beginning, forcing us to recommit and renew our practice and our vows.

This is about the journey, not the destination, I remind myself. It's a way of showing up and being in the world and being honest with myself.

These self-discipline and awareness "muscles" need some exercise to help me move through an area I find myself stuck in - once again. Time to make adjustments, get back in alignment and back on track. And so it is. The practice begins again.

I remind myself to live in the mystery and to remember, "you can make no mistakes."

AFTERWORD

The story of 3:15 began shortly after I left a 16-year marriage and was spending a lot of time by myself in solitude, retreating from the world as I knew it. I suspect that writing and keeping dream journals was a way for me to bear witness to my life and the experiences at a time when I couldn't articulate or share my struggles publicly. It seemed important to write things down, almost as proof to me that my life had value. Perhaps it was an attempt to understand and find some meaning there. I sensed I was going through a pivotal life rebirth. Regardless of what I had accomplished in my outer world, I felt that I was being called upon to experience my internal life in a new way and to be born into greater wisdom, compassion, and usefulness.

The memories I share here aren't necessarily in chronological order. I wrote on whatever notebook or journal was close at hand at the moment. I didn't always take the time to date my entries, because of a sense of urgency I felt I needed to record the details of my experiences while they were still fresh in my mind.

Many of the situations that occurred were beyond my ability to comprehend and they defied probability or logical explanation. These experiences continue to fuel my curiosity. They cause me to dig deeply and look for answers and meaning.

Eventually I came to trust a higher power and honor my soul's journey; I have become comfortable living with mystery.

I'm also something of a compulsive inquisitor. I've read shelves of books and explored ideas, theories, and subjects, ranging from science to spirituality to science fiction and psychology. I love this quote by Einstein from his writing, "What I Believe." He says:

> *"To sense that behind anything that can be experienced there is something that our minds cannot grasp, whose beauty and sublimity reaches us only indirectly, this is religiousness."*

Religiousness for me has been informed through first-hand experience.

My reading and studies include the work of Carl Jung and his theories of synchronicity, along with Jean Shinoda Bolen and Arnold and Amy Mindell's world work, theories of collective consciousness and transpersonal psychology. A Course in Miracles is a part of my life. I reach for the Bible on many occasions. I am touched by Christianity, Hinduism and enfolded in Buddhism. I'm intrigued with quantum physics, string theory, and theories of the continuation of the soul after the death of the physical body. I look for rational explanations, answers and theories, yet remain accepting of not knowing the answers, of living with the questions and living in the mystery.

I've come to revere the practice of meditation. I was baptized Catholic and raised in that tradition. More recently, I've taken vows in Buddhism. I've engaged in numerous silent retreats. The more I research and question, the more I have come to realize that I'm engaged with something that defies a traditional religious belief system. I accept the possibility that I might be receiving guidance or messages from an unknown source or sources. This may explain why it is increasingly important for me to meditate and keep a record through writing and drawing.

These occurrences and experiences are never expected or predictable. They often happen one after another in rapid succession, or they happen in patterns of three, or are repeated multiple times until I acknowledge something significant is happening and trying to get my attention. Paying attention is a skillful means.

Some of these incidents are quite simple, like hearing an obscure song several times in a short period, from a music box, on a car radio, in an elevator, at an airport, or someone's ringtone on a phone. It always seems completely random yet somehow profoundly connected.

While some of my experiences have been alarming and difficult to understand, they are often also funny, weird, and curious. I feel at times I've fallen down a rabbit hole, like Alice, saying to myself, *"Why sometimes I've believed as many as six impossible things before breakfast."*

The questions I find myself asking repeatedly are: What does this mean? Why is this happening? What am I supposed to learn from this? What do I do with this? Where do I go from here?

I continue to seek advice and insight from friends and professionals. Frankly, at times I've been scared and wondered if I'm losing my mind. So I've learned to talk with people I trust. They encourage me to keep writing and using my visual arts practice, to meditate and continue exploring with a curious mind. One of the best pieces of advice I've received is to "live in the mystery." It is this quality of living in the mystery that I embrace today. I've learned to be patient and not act or make decisions about important next steps in my life until I receive a very clear and profound "Yes!" I've also learned the importance of saying no and speaking my truth.

I realize how much these events and adventures have influenced me and the woman I am today, and how they continue to inform my attitude and approach to life.

We share a human capacity to be receivers and transmitters of information through what some would characterize as divine intervention, collective consciousness, or the journey of the soul. As such, I'm grateful for these gifts which propel me to develop an open and curious mind combined with spiritual wonder and belief in the magic inherent in ordinary life.

With curiosity and delight, and by overcoming my own fear and resistance to things beyond my control, the message to me in all of this is: Be aware. Notice things. Put down your electronic devices. Turn off the television and the news. Go outside. Be in nature. Follow the simple signals presented in daily life. Watch, listen, and trust.

As one of my dream messengers told me in a loud voice that woke me from a deep sleep once, "**Margaret! Don't be afraid. You can make no mistakes.**"

POSTSCRIPT

I began compiling my stories for this book in 2015. I couldn't have foreseen a global pandemic would present itself and turn the world as we know it upside down and outside in. As we stay at home, and cars are off the roads, our environment changes -- the air is cleaner. Wildlife is returning to our neighborhoods. A robin makes her nest on the wreath on my front door and I watch her raise five babies and teach them to fly and leave the nest.

I ride my bicycle every day. It's as if I've taken a giant step back to the 1950's when life was so much simpler. For 60 consecutive days I cook every meal for myself - something I've never done in my life. I start my flowers from seed and tend them through the spring and summer thanks to the stay at home order. My garden has never looked more beautiful. I adorn the fence on my patio with my artwork and spend my mornings there working on my laptop and notice the bumblebees on the sunflowers; dragonflies, butterflies and hummingbirds bring me joy.

I start a mending basket and darn the holes in my socks while I watch TV in the evening -- just like my mother used to do! I purchase a sewing machine from Amazon and begin to make face coverings from my stash of souvenir tee-shirts I never wear. I read two or three books a week and add a little library to my front yard to recycle books with my neighbors. Jack, my 16-year-old Tibetan Terrier is delighted he's getting walked three times a day.

I walk seven doors down to my daughter's house to share coffee in the morning before the heat of the day in July. My grandson and I watch Patriot Act in the evening and make art in my basement studio. Life is good."

We must live in the mystery as this continues to unfold. And we must stand up and be bold in our collective call to action. We must be determined to fight for the rights of all people across the world and the future of our planet. There is a renewed ealization that nothing is more important than human connection and our elationships with one another. In the words of Martin Luther King, Jr., ***"Only through an inner spiritual transformation do we gain the strength to fight vigorously the evils of the world in a humble and loving spirit. This hour of history needs a dedicated circle of transformed noncomformists."***

ACKNOWLEDGEMENTS

Without my muse and niece, Elise, this book would never have been completed. Our time together has been filled with crackerjack conversations and deliberations, laughter, travel and amazing food. Mmmmm, black truffle risotto in Croatia!

I would like to express my sincere sense of indebtedness for the deeply cherished friendships of Cathy Pace-Pequeno, Jeanna Player, Deborah Nourse, Pamela and Kristin Razecca, Pam Jowett, Gayle Masters, Judy Malouf, Anne Cullimore Decker, Nora Wood, Richard Brown, Suzanne Sullivan, Emily Mason Beard, Pat Martin, Diane Stewart, Lynnette Hiskey, Leanna Clark, Nicole Foster, Bill Foster and Marck Foster.

I also want to acknowledge my brothers and sisters, Jim, Bob, Tom, John, Joe, Mary, Tim and Barbara for putting up with me, testing my patience and driving me to persist.

I thank all of the many colleagues I've had the privilege of working with and learning from over these years at the Salt Palace, Utah Power, PacifiCorp, Naropa, Salt Lake City, the State of Utah and the State of Colorado.

Beyond this I have had the blessings of many great teachers. I continue to be inspired and learn from them. I especially appreciate the writers: Anne Waldman and her lavish use of the red pen critique on my writing, Leland Williams and Joan

Anderson for their encouragement and support of my creative expression from my days at Naropa.

There are a few friends that had a profound influence at pivotal moments in my life I haven't acknowledged.

Stephen Goldsmith told me once that he thought I was a "Buddhist at heart" at a time I expressed my disappointment with the limitations of organized religion. He recommended I read *A Path With Heart* by Jack Kornfield. This book became both a touchstone and a turning point in my spiritual quest. My copy of this book is dog eared and treasured. When I participate in meditation workshops with Jack Kornfield, or hear his voice on a meditation tape, I feel as if once again, I've come home to myself.

David Sisam's friendship, humor and honesty about wanting me to be happy and asking "what are you waiting for?" was another turning point in my life. His gift of *A Course in Miracles* took me further into my exploration of everyday miracles and connected me more deeply to an inner voice, or the Holy Spirit, a familiar concept from my Catholic start in life.

The spiritual pilgrimage with Marianne Williamson introduced me to a powerful, fearless woman, a determined leader, role model and friend. I have given her brilliant book, *A Return to Love* as a gift to many friends. When my daughter Nicole and I participated in a writing workshop with Marianne and Balboa Press in San Francisco, I was encouraged to write this book. Her kick-ass courage and authentic voice continues to inspire me.

Mother Meera's appearance in my dream and my pilgrimage provided me the gifts of radical trust and protection.

David Whyte's poetry and wisdom connected me to the idea of living an art-filled life and the power of words in the soul's journey, and to discover the courage to say no and the wisdom to wait for yes.

Theresa Holleran's validation of my experiences allowed me to remain curious and to honor the mysteries of synchronicity and the challenges of my life.

Governors Jon Huntsman and Gary Herbert gave me the opportunity to be in service in Utah. Governors John Hickenlooper and Jared Polis gave me the opportunity to be of service in Colorado.

And finally, and most importantly, my daughter, Nicole Foster; my life would have been unfulfilled without you and your presence. You have my utmost respect and love. Thanks for your friendship.

I hold sincere gratitude for each and every person and experience I've had along this amazing journey, so far. To be continued.

DISCUSSION QUESTIONS FOR THE READER

Chapter 1 - Beginning

There is much we can learn about ourselves from looking back at our childhood. Each experience we've had has imprinted itself on us along our personal journey, whether we are consciously aware of it or not. Take a few minutes to think back to your earliest years and try to determine some significant events and how they may have shaped you or influenced your thinking as the person you are today.

- What are some of your earliest childhood memories?
- What made these events so significant in your life?
- How have these memories and experiences impacted you emotionally or mentally? Are they positive, and do they keep you moving forward, or are they something you need to make amends with and release? Are they holding you back?

Chapter 2 – Dream Angels

Dream states have been described as being "a window into the subconscious mind." Research shows that our minds never actually turn off, but go into different levels of brainwave activity throughout different times of the day. In being more consciously aware of the power of your dreams through recording and analyzing them, you may be able identify and answer some questions about yourself, your relationships, or your professional life which will assist you on your path forward.

- When you dream, do you have frequent recurring themes, such as flying or running?
- Do you have intense emotions while you sleep, or do you wake often throughout the night?
- How do your dreams affect your waking life? Do you notice that you are sometimes in a good mood or a bad mood, or experience anxiety, depending on the dreams you had?
- Has there been a period in your life when your dream state has been more active than usual? Do you recall that period and what was happening in your life at that time?
- What are your bedtime routines? Activities that occur within 30 minutes of sleep can affect your sleep quality as well as dream states, so be intentional about nighttime activities.
- Do you keep a dream journal? Sometimes patterns become more apparent when a body of dreams is explored.

Chapter 3 – Make Believe

Our formative years generally consist of our upbringing, family and home life, and schooling. However, the period when we first begin to develop into our own unique individuals has an important impact on us and who we decide to become. Think back to when you first started making decisions for yourself, and consider what it was that drove you to make those specific choices.

- Do you remember the name of your first best friend? How old were you? What do you remember about this person and your friendship with them?
- Do you remember your first act of disobedience? What was it, and why do you think it was important for you to rebel at that particular time?

Chapter 4 – Wake Up

When we're able to look at our lives as a big picture or "whole," it becomes easier to decode some of the meaning behind certain things that have happened to us and the experiences we've had. Similar to when we are searching for answers and they suddenly appear in front of us, we can also listen for answers from external sources that speak from within ourselves. When we take the time to step back from our present mindset and assess each area of our life, it is easier to recognize the signs and pivot points that will help us navigate our journey.

- Have you ever experienced synchronicity or meaningful coincidences in your life? If so, what were they? Did you detect any significance or meaning in them?
- Were they important at the time, or did they help you discover answers or direction in your life?

Chapter 5 – Time

Just as Einstein stated in his early works, time is relative. That is, the rate at which it passes is dependent on the frame of reference of the observer. In some Buddhist teachings, it's suggested that without conditioning, the concept of time ceases to exist; that there is no time, and without time there is no present, no past, and no future. Depending on how we embrace and utilize it, it can seem that time stands still, moves in slow motion, or can be gone in the blink of an eye.

- How do you view time? What role does it play in your life?
- Do you believe you are dedicating a healthy amount of time to each critical area of life, such as health, career or productivity, relationships, and education?
- Do you notice yourself constantly watching the clock, waiting for the next deadline or 'thing' to happen? How can you adjust your relationship with time to be more present and in the moment?
- Are their activities you engage in when it feels as though time stands still? What are those activities?
- What do you consider your most valuable time? Is it spent with family or friends, exploring nature, or being creative? What value does that bring to you, and why?

Chapter 6 – Love

Our connections with other people are arguably the most critical factors in long term health and happiness. Whether our relationships are with friends, family members, or romantic partners, it is important that we nurture these connections. Other people can help us gain a clearer perspective on who we are, what we need, and whether we are heading in the right direction and being true to ourselves. While some relationships are life-long, others are short-term and we move on when that relationship feels "complete."

- Has a close friend or colleague asked you a personal question that gave you pause to think deeply about yourself or your life?
- Have you ever been confronted with a life-altering decision that you knew you had to make, but lacked the courage or motivation needed to take the next step?
- What relationships are most valuable to you in your life? Are you taking the time to show appreciation and gratitude for those people?

Chapter 7 – Transitions

No matter what a person's background or socio-economic level is, most everyone goes through similar stages or phases throughout their life. When we're faced with the changing "seasons of life," it's imperative that we keep our minds and hearts open to messages and ideas from varying sources. For some people those may often come through written words, while others glean insight from artistic endeavors, meditation, or interaction with friends. Keep yourself open, especially at these times in life, and be ready to examine what is presented to you.

- Is there a mentor, artist, or author whose work has had a significant impact on your thoughts or life?
- When at a pivotal moment or period of change in your life, do you open yourself to the unknown or close yourself off and shut down? Why?
- Do you take time to be alone with yourself and your thoughts? How often do you take time to reflect on your current emotional, mental and spiritual state?

Chapter 8 – The Gift

Messages, clues, and hints can appear to us in many ways. Our connections with others as well as ourselves can help bring clarity around these insightful messages we receive. When faced with challenges and obstacles in life, one of the most valuable resources we have is our ability to recognize the signs that are pointing us in a direction of answers and assistance. The more we open our minds and hearts to accept these indicators, the more easily they will flow to us.

- Was there ever a time that your thoughts or feelings were validated by a book or voice of another? What connection did you find between the two?
- Who in your life do you look towards to help you sort through difficult situations or obstacles?
- Have you had prophetic dreams, or, have incidents in your dreams foreshadowed of events that were about to occur?

Chapter 9 – Journey

Each of us is on our own personal journey in life - here to learn what we're meant to learn through the advancement of our souls. Throughout our lives we gain valuable insight that we take with us into the next period or chapter of our story. Sometimes things seem to click and fall into place easily, and other times we may have to put much more intensive efforts into the meaning of our life or arriving at some particular destination. When we recognize that all things that happen to us are an important part of our journey, we can more easily enjoy the experience and let go of any fear of the unknown.

- This chapter delves into the practice of meditation. Do you practice meditation? When did you begin, and why? How did you learn? Is there a particular style of meditation you practice such as closed eyes, open eyes, using a mantra, etc?
- Have you ever made any important decision based on instinct or intuition? What do you think the reason was that you felt you were directed to do something?
- How often do you see signs and synchronicities in your life? Do you accept the messages that are presenting themselves to you?

Chapter 10- Darshan

Every person on this planet has a distinct personal DNA. While your chemical makeup is unique to you, every part of the current whole also existed long before you did. Think about your natural talents and gifts and consider where they possibly came from. Perhaps those skills that you are blessed with today may have been passed down from people who lived centuries before you came into this world.

- Have you researched your family history and ancestry? If so, how did it impact the person you are or believed yourself to be? If not, do you think this knowledge may add value to your life? Why or why not?
- How do you think your ancestral past may have affected you or your life experiences?
- Has there ever been a time in your life that you made a decision based on intuition or 'gut-feeling,' and if so, what opportunities did it open or path did it lead you down?

Chapter 11 – Protection

Every one of us has likely dealt with trauma of some kind. Trauma can be mental, physical or emotional. As children, we're likely protected by our parents. But that isn't always the case. Protection seems to occur at the gateway between innocence and self-empowerment, or the establishment of our will.

- Have you ever felt a compelling need for protection from something or someone? What was that situation?
- For women readers, did your father influence your choice in lovers and life partners?
- For men, did your mother influence your choice in lovers and life partners?
- Was there a time in your life when you were publicly shamed for one of your actions or choices? What was it? How did you deal with it?

- Have you ever experienced depression or been in a position of supporting a family member or friend dealing with depression?
- What have you learned from these life experiences and how have they made you a stronger person today?

Chapter 12 – Home

Your personal feeling or sense of 'home' may be entirely different than another person's. When most people think of home, they think of a place where they lay their head at night. But a feeling of belonging or connection can oftentimes give us even more comfort than a physical space. Imagine your relationship with your spouse, a close friend, or even your parents. Although there may be a physical place associated with these relationships, the feeling of solace from these connections are truly what gives us the peace of mind and familiarity.

- Have you moved and changed homes frequently in your life? What was the reason or reasons?
- What did you learn from moving?
- Has a colleague or friend reappeared in your life unexpectedly? Why do you think that happened?
- Do you ever find yourself asking, who am I? Where do I belong? What should I be doing with my life?

Chapter 13 – Peyote Medicine

There are times in life that we are faced with experiences that we could never predict and hardly believe we experienced once we look back at them. It is important to remember that each and every interaction we have with others always brings some meaning or insight with it. Sometimes we must give to the other person, whether it be advice or a smile or encouragement, and other times we are meant to receive something.

- When was the last time you made a meaningful connection with a stranger? What impact did it have on you, and what impact do you think it had on the other person?
- Have you ever stopped to assist a stranger on the side of the road or the sidewalk?

Chapter 14 – Synchronicity

Synchronicity refers to events that appear to be meaningful coincidences in our lives. They seem to occur with no causal relationship yet they seem to be significantly related for some reason.

- Have you experienced synchronicity in your life?
- Have you ever consulted with a professional about your life experiences and the challenges you are facing?
- Has someone close to you died and did you experience a connection with that person after he/she passed over?
- Have you ever heard a voice inside your head giving you direction or guidance?
- Has someone randomly appeared and come to your assistance when you need them?

Chapter 15 – Creativity

Creative pursuits are a natural way that we can express our emotions and deal with challenges in life. It's important for us to nurture our creative side and let things flow out of us without logic or reason. Think about how children are so free with their creative expressions and let their imaginations run wild. As adults, unfortunately we seem to put these things lower on our priority list, but it's easy to make a positive change in this area of life. For some people, working with their hands may be therapeutic, while others appreciate working with their minds. No matter the craft, make it a priority to engage in some form of artistic or creative activities on a regular basis.

- Is there an activity you lose track of time when you are engaged in? What is it?
- When you were a child, what types of activities and fun things did you enjoy doing most?
- How did you envision yourself and your life when you were growing up?
- What age were you when you faced the first great challenge of your life? What was it?
- Do you have a creative pursuit? What is it?

Chapter 16 – Alchemy

Although we are alone on our respective individual journeys, we are also very much all connected. A general belief is that people in all parts of the world are connected by fields of energy. Some spiritual practices and religious views hold the belief that there is one collective consciousness that each and every one of us is a part of, and therefore we are all connected to one another.

- Have you ever experienced the sense of being part of a greater field of awareness? Can you describe it?
- Do you pay attention to external signs and world events to reflect on its significance to your life or inner world?

Chapter 17 – Discovery

The process of discovery requires us to let go of what we think we know. It often entails radical trust that the Universe will provide for us and we don't have to know the answers. Through discovery, we follow a path less traveled which can lead to a future greater for ourselves different than what we've imagined.

- How do you respond when someone calls you for help? Do you experience conflicting reactions?
- Has helping someone else ever resulted in discovering something wonderful for yourself?
- Have you ever relied on radical trust or waited for a clear "Yes" when making an important life decision? What was the reasoning behind it and the result?

Chapter 18 – Letting Go

Most of us spend the majority of our lives acquiring things-education, experiences, and material possessions. But there comes a time when we may step back and see all of these things as burdens, obligations, or figurative weight that we are carrying around. Instead of constantly pushing ourselves to gain, at times it is good to release some of what we have, especially if it is holding us back from progressing forward.

- Have you gone through the process of letting go of your things and your identity? How did it feel, and what was the end result?
- Was there any time in your life that you wanted to shed some pieces of your past? If so, what were those pieces and what was the process like for you?
- What did letting go contribute to you and your life? What impact did it have?

Chapter 19 – The Voice

Each and every one of us has what is known as intuition, gut feeling, or instincts. Although this super power exists in all of us, some people function on a higher frequency or higher level than others. Why is this? Some may say it is a natural ability while others believe that it is a skill you are able to develop and improve with practice. No matter your belief on this topic, make it a point to listen closely to your inner voice and pay special attention when you believe a message is trying to make its way to you.

- What does "You Can Make No Mistakes" mean to you?
- Have you taken breaks from electronic devices? Is this a regular practice? Why or why not?
- The author speaks about finding her voice; have you struggled to find your voice? How did you resolve this?
- The author addresses the difference between the voice of the ego and the voice of the Higher Self. What does this mean to you? Do you see the distinction between the two?

Chapter 20 – Surrender

It is said that most ailments, problems, and causes of stress in this world exist solely in an individual's mind. Research shows that the symptoms of a disease become noticeably more intense and detrimental after diagnosis. Why do you think that is? Is it possible that most of the difficult issues we face in life are a result of the way we think? When we untangle the litany that may be fogging up our minds, we start to see our reality with more clarity, positivity, and gratitude.

- Have you experienced a situation that was challenging where you found that relinquishing control was the best choice for you?
- What does the concept of surrender mean to you?
- Do you have experience of surrendering and letting go? What was that experience? What was the outcome?

Chapter 21 – Illusions

The author retells the story of seeing the same scene from a movie over and over again. The synchronicity of the repetitive scene has a profound impact because of the question as to whether we truly have control and the loss of control.

- What does it mean to you to give up the illusion of control?
- Can you describe a time you did and what the results were?

- What kinds of illusions do you hold onto? Is the illusion of control one of them?
- How did the global pandemic, (COVID-19) alter your perceptions of being in control of your life?

Chapter 22 – Fields

The author speaks of fields of consciousness, where people have the same thoughts and ideas across space and time.
- Have you had the experience of thinking about someone and your phone rings and they are calling you? Do you remember the details?
- Have you ever found that you and someone close to you were doing the same thing at the same time, like the author's experience of watching a movie only to discover her daughter was watching the same movie at the same time in a different location?
- What do you think about the concept of fields of consciousness or collective consciousness?

Chapter 23 - Service

Paying it forward and giving back to the community plays a pivotal role in health, wealth, and abundance in our lives. Even when we feel we're at a low point, doing for others takes our minds off of ourselves, adds value to our feelings of self-worth, and may also make a positive impact on others. One of the best ways we can be of service in our lives is to connect with causes and charities that are important to us or have had an impact on our lives. Take time to connect yourself with local or global initiatives that resonate with you and make a conscious effort to spread awareness, volunteer, or give back in some way.

- Has public service played a role in your life? If so, how, and what was the impact it had on you?
- Have you discovered quiet and mighty companions in your life? Who are they and how did they present themselves?
- What causes and initiatives are most meaningful to you, and why?
- Are you being in service to others as much as you can?

Chapter 24 – Digging Deeper

Life is cyclical. Valuable lessons are always presenting themselves to us throughout our lives. There are times we may be faced with the same obstacles and challenges we've had to deal with before. This often means that it's time to relearn the same lesson again or re-evaluate ourselves and our situations.

- The author suggests that life is a cycle, or a spiral, with constant relearning and recommitment to spiritual practice rather than an upward linear path. What repeated pitfalls have you experienced in your life that have led to a renewed commitment to your practices?
- Have you felt a greater sense of confidence and fearlessness in your life as a result of the challenges you faced? Is there a pivotal moment you can recall?
- Do you have close friends and family you call upon when you need support in your life?

BIBGLIOGRAPHY & RECOMMENDED READING

Chapter 4 – Wake Up
Lightman, Alan, *Einstein's Dreams* (Vintage Books, a division of Random House) 1993

Chapter 5 - Time
Taylor, Jeremy, *Dream Work Toolkit*
International Association for the Study of Dreams, www.asdreams.org

Chapter 6 - The Gift
Meera, Mother, *Bringing Down the Light*, 1990, www.mothermeera.com
King Jr., Martin Luther, *Faith is Taking the First Step* (Paraphrased) The King Center
Polar Express, Film by Robert Zemeckis and William Broyles 2004. Based on the children's book by Chris Van Allsburg

Chapter 7 – Journey
Aurobindo, Sri, *The Mother* (Lotus Light Publications) 1995
The Holy Bible St. Joseph New Catholic Edition (Catholic Book Publishing Co) 1962

Chapter 9 – Protection
Bolen, Jean Shinoda, *Tao of Psychology: Synchronicity & the Self*
(Harper/San Francisco) 1982

Chapter 10 – Home
Chopra, Deepak, *Quantum Healing* (Bantam Books) 1989,
www.deepakchopra.com

Chapter 13 – Love
Williamson, Marianne *A Return to Love* (Harper Perennial)
1993, www.marianne.com
Whyte, David, *The Heart Aroused* (Doubleday) 1996, www.
davidwhyte.com
A Course in Miracles (Foundation for Inner Peace) 1975, www.
acim.org/acim/

Chapter 14 - Transitions
Campbell, Joseph, *The Hero's Journey*
Whyte, David, *The Heart Aroused* (Doubleday) 1996

Chapter 15 - Creativity
Rumi, Jalal ad-Din Muhammad (1207-1273)

Chapter 16 – Alchemy
McKenna, Terrance 1946-2000

Chapter 17 - Discovery
Overton, Patrick, *The Leaning Tree, Poems*

Chapter 19 - The Voice
Whyte, David, *"The Well of Grief"*

Chapter 20 - Illusions
Instinct (Touchstone Pictures/Spyglass Entertainment) 1999

Chapter 21 - Fields
Nolan, Christopher, *Interstellar* (2014)

Afterword
Carroll, Lewis, *Through the Looking Glass* (1871)

Postscript
King, Martin Luther Jr. *Strength to Love*